Salad Days

THE AUSTRALIAN Women's Weekly

contents

Forget the weather, or the season — any day and almost any time of the day is right for a delicious, nutritious salad. Most of the recipes for starters can double as main courses, and some of the main course salads would make wonderful starters or light meals — simply serve less than we suggest.

Pamela Clark
Food Director

starters

Start with a bang...juicy mango, fresh prawns and garlic chicken whet the appetite and, while small servings and light dressings leave room for the main event, many of these starters will also make great main courses.

crab and green papaya salad

400g cooked crab meat, shredded
1 medium green papaya (350g), grated coarsely
½ cup (50g) coarsely grated fresh coconut
½ cup coarsely chopped fresh mint
1 fresh small red thai chilli, chopped finely
18 large betel leaves
coconut dressing
1 tablespoon peanut oil
1 tablespoon lime juice
2 tablespoons coconut cream
2 teaspoons fish sauce

1 Make coconut dressing.
2 Combine crab, papaya, coconut, mint, chilli and dressing in medium bowl.
3 Divide crab mixture among betel leaves.
coconut dressing Combine ingredients in screw-top jar; shake well.
prep time *20 minutes* **serves** *6*
nutritional count per serving *7.3g total fat (3.9g saturated fat); 456kJ (129 cal); 4.6g carbohydrate; 10g protein; 2.8g fibre*

To open fresh coconut, pierce one of the eyes then roast coconut briefly in a very hot oven only until cracks appear in the shell. Cool the coconut, then break it apart and grate the flesh.

4

avocado and prawn salad

12 uncooked large king prawns (840g)
¾ cup (50g) stale breadcrumbs
2 tablespoons finely grated parmesan cheese
1 teaspoon finely grated lime rind
2 tablespoons plain flour
1 egg, beaten lightly
vegetable oil, for shallow-frying
60g baby spinach leaves
3 medium avocados (750g), sliced thickly
1 fresh long red chilli, chopped finely
chilli lime mayonnaise
½ cup (150g) mayonnaise
1 fresh small red thai chilli, chopped finely
1 tablespoon lime juice

For stale breadcrumbs, grate, blend or process one- or two-day-old white bread. This makes a fluffier crumb than packaged breadcrumbs, and it is perfect for mixing with other similar-sized ingredients like the grated cheese in this recipe.
For shallow-frying, use enough oil to reach half-way up the food; cook until brown and crisp, then turn over and cook the other side.

1 Make chilli lime mayonnaise.
2 Shell and devein prawns, leaving tails intact.
3 Combine breadcrumbs, cheese and rind in medium bowl. Coat prawns in flour; shake off excess. Dip in egg, then coat in breadcrumb mixture.
4 Heat oil in wok; shallow-fry prawns, in batches, until browned lightly. Drain on absorbent paper.
5 Divide spinach among plates; top with avocado and prawns, sprinkle over chilli then drizzle with mayonnaise.
chilli lime mayonnaise Combine ingredients in small bowl.
prep and cook time *40 minutes* **serves** *6*
nutritional count per serving *36.6g total fat (6.7g saturated fat); 1768kJ (423 cal); 13.9g carbohydrate; 19.9g protein; 2.3g fibre*

soba salad with rocket and mandarin

180g soba noodles

2 medium mandarins (400g),
    segmented, chopped coarsely

2 green onions, sliced thinly

½ cup (80g) roasted pine nuts

40g baby rocket leaves

mandarin vinaigrette

¼ cup (60ml) olive oil

¼ cup (60ml) mandarin juice

1 tablespoon rice wine vinegar

1 Cook noodles in medium saucepan of boiling water, uncovered, until tender; drain. Rinse under cold water; drain.

2 Meanwhile, make mandarin vinaigrette.

3 Combine noodles and dressing in large bowl with remaining ingredients.

mandarin vinaigrette Combine ingredients in screw-top jar; shake well.

prep and cook time 20 minutes **serves** 6

nutritional count per serving 18.9g total fat (1.9g saturated fat); 1262kJ (302 cal); 26g carbohydrate; 5.8g protein; 2.8g fibre

minted crab and cucumber salad

500g cooked crab meat, shredded

¼ cup coarsely chopped fresh coriander

¼ cup coarsely chopped fresh mint

2 lebanese cucumbers (260g), sliced into ribbons

15g baby mizuna leaves

chilli lime dressing

¼ cup (60ml) lime juice

1 tablespoon light soy sauce

1 tablespoon peanut oil

2 teaspoons grated palm sugar

1 fresh long red chilli, chopped finely

1 clove garlic, crushed

1 Make chilli lime dressing.

2 Combine crab, herbs and dressing in medium bowl; toss gently.

3 Divide cucumber among serving plates; top with crab mixture and mizuna.

chilli lime dressing Combine ingredients in screw-top jar; shake well.

prep time 15 minutes **serves** 10

nutritional count per serving 2.2g total fat (0.4g saturated fat); 234kJ (56 cal); 2.1g carbohydrate; 6.7g protein; 0.5g fibre

You need two punnets of baby mizuna for this recipe. Large mizuna leaves can be used instead. Use drained, canned crab meat, or flesh from cooked crabs. You can also buy fresh crab meat from the fish markets.

antipasto salad with hummus dressing

6 baby eggplants (360g), halved lengthways
1 tablespoon olive oil
6 slices prosciutto (90g)
1 cup (150g) drained semi-dried tomatoes in oil
1 cup (120g) seeded black olives
6 bocconcini cheese (360g)
1 tablespoon whole fresh flat-leaf parsley leaves
30g radicchio leaves
30g baby rocket leaves
12 grissini (80g)
hummus dressing
⅓ cup (65g) dried chickpeas
1 clove garlic, quartered
2 tablespoons lemon juice
2 teaspoons tahini
2 teaspoons olive oil

Use a 400g can of rinsed, drained chickpeas in place of the dried chickpeas, or buy ready-made hummus from delis or supermarkets. You will need to buy one small radicchio to get the amount of leaves required for this recipe.

1 Make hummus dressing.
2 Preheat oven to 220°C/200°C fan-forced.
3 Combine eggplant and oil in small bowl. Cook eggplant, in batches, on heated grill plate (or grill or barbecue) until browned.
4 Place prosciutto, in single layer, on baking-paper-lined oven tray; top with another sheet of baking paper. Cover with a similar-sized oven tray to flatten prosciutto. Cook, in oven, about 10 minutes or until prosciutto is crisp.
5 Divide tomato, olives, cheese, parsley, radicchio, rocket, prosciutto and eggplant among plates; drizzle with dressing. Serve with grissini.
hummus dressing Place chickpeas in medium bowl, cover with cold water; stand overnight. Drain chickpeas, place in small saucepan; cover with cold water. Bring to the boil; simmer, covered, about 50 minutes or until chickpeas are tender. Drain chickpeas over small heatproof bowl. Reserve ¼ cup cooking liquid; discard remaining liquid. Blend or process chickpeas with garlic, juice, tahini, oil and reserved cooking liquid until almost smooth.
prep and cook time 1 hour 20 minutes (+ standing) *serves* 6
nutritional count per serving 19.3g total fat (7.5g saturated fat); 1601kJ (383 cal); 28.1g carbohydrate; 20.6g protein; 7.7g fibre

broad bean and goats cheese salad

1 teaspoon ground cumin
1 teaspoon ground coriander
½ teaspoon ground fennel
½ teaspoon hot paprika
⅓ cup (55g) almond kernels
1 egg white, beaten lightly
1 cup (120g) fresh or frozen shelled broad beans
1 stalk celery (150g), trimmed, sliced thinly
½ cup loosely packed fresh mint leaves
½ small red onion (50g), sliced thinly
120g soft goats cheese, crumbled
minted lime dressing
¼ cup (60ml) olive oil
1 tablespoon lime juice
1 tablespoon finely chopped fresh mint

1 Preheat oven to 200°C/180°C fan-forced. Grease and line oven tray with baking paper.
2 Combine spices in small shallow bowl. Dip nuts in egg white then in spice mixture to coat; place on oven tray.
3 Roast nuts about 10 minutes, stirring occasionally, until browned; cool.
4 Meanwhile, make minted lime dressing.
5 Combine beans, celery, mint, onion and dressing in medium serving bowl; sprinkle with nuts and cheese.
minted lime dressing Combine ingredients in screw-top jar; shake well.
***prep and cook time** 30 minutes **serves** 4*
***nutritional count per serving** 27g total fat (5g saturated fat); 1254kJ (300 cal); 2.8g carbohydrate; 10.2g protein; 4g fibre*

salmon ceviche salad

2 medium oranges (480g)
400g piece sashimi-quality salmon, sliced thinly
175g watercress, trimmed
orange and dill dressing
1 tablespoon white wine vinegar
1 tablespoon rinsed, drained baby capers
2 teaspoons finely chopped fresh dill

1 Segment oranges over small bowl; reserve ¼ cup orange juice for the vinaigrette.
2 Make orange and dill vinaigrette.
3 Combine salmon and half the dressing in medium bowl; stand 5 minutes.
4 Combine salmon mixture with remaining dressing, watercress and orange segments in large serving bowl.
orange and dill dressing Combine vinegar, capers, dill and reserved juice in screw-top jar; shake well.
***prep time** 25 minutes **serves** 4*
***nutritional count per serving** 7.3g total fat (1.6g saturated fat); 773kJ (185 cal); 7.4g carbohydrate; 21g protein; 2.6g fibre*

Use the freshest, sashimi-quality fish you can find. Raw fish sold as sashimi has to meet stringent guidelines regarding its handling and treatment after leaving the water. We suggest you seek local advice from authorities before eating any raw seafood.

Ceviche, pronounced
se-vee-chay, is a Latin-
American specialty.
The acids in the citrus
marinade slightly cook
the very thinly sliced
raw seafood.

crispy duck with pomegranate salad

2 duck breast fillets (300g), skin on
¼ teaspoon dried chilli flakes
¼ teaspoon sea salt flakes
¼ cup (60ml) orange juice
2 tablespoons balsamic vinegar
1 tablespoon wholegrain mustard
½ teaspoon honey
1 cup (80g) bean sprouts
½ cup (125ml) pomegranate pulp
30g baby spinach leaves, sliced finely
½ cup firmly packed fresh mint leaves

You need to buy a medium pomegranate (320g) to get ½ cup pulp. To remove the pulp from the pomegranate, cut it in half, then hit the back of the fruit with a wooden spoon – the seeds usually fall out easily. Discard the shell and white pith.

1 Remove excess fat from duck breasts; rub duck with combined chilli and salt. Prick duck skins with fork several times. Cook duck, skin-side down, in heated oiled medium frying pan about 8 minutes or until crisp. Turn duck; cook about 5 minutes or until cooked as desired. Cover duck; stand 5 minutes then slice thinly.
2 Meanwhile, combine juice, vinegar, mustard and honey in same cleaned pan; simmer, uncovered, about 2 minutes or until sauce is reduced by half.
3 Combine remaining ingredients in medium bowl; divide among serving plates. Top salad with duck; drizzle with orange sauce.
prep and cook time 30 minutes **serves** 4
nutritional count per serving 28g total fat (8.3g saturated fat); 1375kJ (329 cal); 6.9g carbohydrate; 11.6g protein; 3.4g fibre

parsnip, pear and blue cheese salad

1 small parsnip (120g)
vegetable oil, for deep-frying
40g baby rocket leaves
120g fresh raspberries
1 medium pear (230g), sliced thinly
100g soft blue cheese, cut lengthways
   into four slices
raspberry vinaigrette
⅓ cup (80ml) olive oil
2 tablespoons raspberry vinegar

1 Using vegetable peeler, cut parsnip into long, thin strips.
2 Heat oil in medium deep saucepan; deep-fry parsnip, in batches, until browned lightly. Drain on absorbent paper.
3 Make raspberry vinaigrette.
4 Combine rocket, raspberries and pear with vinaigrette in large serving bowl; top with cheese and parsnip.
raspberry vinaigrette Combine ingredients in screw-top jar; shake well.
prep and cook time 20 minutes **serves** *4*
nutritional count per serving *28g total fat (7.9g saturated fat); 1371kJ (328 cal); 11.7g carbohydrate; 6.3g protein; 3.8g fibre*

lemon garlic chicken salad on ciabatta

1 litre (4 cups) water
400g chicken breast fillets
4 thick slices ciabatta bread (140g)
1 tablespoon olive oil
1 clove garlic, crushed
lemon, chilli and parsley dressing
2 tablespoons olive oil
2 teaspoons finely grated lemon rind
1 fresh long red chilli, chopped finely
2 tablespoons finely chopped fresh
   flat-leaf parsley

1 Bring the water to the boil in large frying pan; add chicken. Reduce heat; simmer, covered, about 10 minutes or until chicken is cooked. Cool chicken in poaching liquid 10 minutes; drain, shred chicken finely.
2 Meanwhile, preheat grill to hot.
3 Brush bread both sides with combined oil and garlic; toast, both sides, under grill.
4 Make lemon, chilli and parsley dressing.
5 Combine chicken and dressing in large bowl; divide among toasts.
lemon, chilli and parsley dressing Combine ingredients in screw-top jar; shake well.
prep and cook time 15 minutes **serves** *4*
nutritional count per serving *20.1g total fat (3.8g saturated fat); 1438kJ (344 cal); 15.8g carbohydrate; 24.5g protein; 1.3g fibre*

For best results when deep-frying, check the oil is hot enough before adding the parsnip strips. Dip the handle end of a wooden spoon into the hot oil, if bubbles immediately form around the wood, the oil is the correct temperature.

fennel and ruby red grapefruit salad

2 ruby red grapefruit (700g)
1 medium fennel bulb (300g), trimmed,
   sliced thinly
2 stalks celery (300g), trimmed, sliced thinly
1 cup loosely packed fresh flat-leaf parsley leaves
¼ cup (25g) roasted walnut halves
white balsamic vinaigrette
¼ cup (60ml) olive oil
1 tablespoon white balsamic vinegar

1 Segment grapefruit over small bowl; reserve
2 tablespoons juice for vinaigrette.
2 Make white balsamic vinaigrette.
3 Combine grapefruit, vinaigrette and remaining
ingredients in medium serving bowl.
white balsamic vinaigrette Combine oil, vinegar
and reserved juice in screw-top jar; shake well.
prep time *20 minutes* ***serves*** *4*
nutritional count per serving *18.3g total fat*
(2.2g saturated fat); 890kJ (213 cal);
7.7g carbohydrate; 2.9g protein; 3.9g fibre

smoked salmon salad with tamarind dressing

2 lebanese cucumbers (260g)
200g sliced smoked salmon
1 medium avocado (250g), halved, sliced thinly
2 green onions, sliced thinly
1 tablespoon sesame seeds, toasted
tamarind dressing
1 tablespoon light soy sauce
1 tablespoon water
1 tablespoon brown sugar
2 teaspoons tamarind concentrate
1 teaspoon fish sauce
1 teaspoon olive oil
1cm piece fresh ginger (5g), grated
1 clove garlic, crushed

1 Make tamarind dressing.
2 Using vegetable peeler, slice unpeeled cucumber
into long, thin strips.
3 Divide salmon, cucumber, avocado and onion
among serving plates; sprinkle with sesame seeds,
drizzle with dressing.
tamarind dressing Combine ingredients in small
saucepan; stir over heat, without boiling, until
sugar dissolves, cool.
prep and cook time *15 minutes* ***serves*** *6*
nutritional count per serving *10.1g total fat*
(2g saturated fat); 640kJ (153 cal);
5g carbohydrate; 9.7g protein; 2g fibre

Instead of coriander, try thai basil; it has a strong basil flavour and is an almost indispensible ingredient in Thai cooking. It is also said to bring good fortune.

coconut lobster with herbed salad

2 cooked large lobsters (2.5kg)
100g dried thin rice stick noodles
⅔ cup loosely packed fresh coriander leaves
⅔ cup loosely packed fresh mint leaves
chilli coconut dressing
200ml coconut cream
1 tablespoon hot chilli sauce
1 tablespoon lime juice
2 teaspoons fish sauce
2 fresh kaffir lime leaves, torn

Prawn or crab meat can be used instead of lobster.

1 Make chilli coconut dressing.
2 Meanwhile, discard heads from lobsters. Using scissors, cut away soft shell from under lobster tails, then pull away hard shells. Cut lobster flesh into 1cm slices; combine with dressing.
3 Place noodles in medium heatproof bowl, cover with boiling water; stand until tender, drain. Rinse under cold water; drain.
4 Divide noodles among serving plates; top with lobster mixture, sprinkle with combined remaining ingredients.
chilli coconut dressing Combine ingredients in small saucepan; bring to the boil. Reduce heat; simmer, uncovered, 2 minutes. Strain dressing into medium heatproof bowl; discard solids. Cool 20 minutes.
prep and cook time *25 minutes (+ cooling)* ***serves*** *6*
nutritional count per serving *8.4g total fat (6.3g saturated fat); 1049kJ (251 cal); 13.1g carbohydrate; 29.7g protein; 1.5g fibre*

Mushrooms are grown in a hygienic environment, so there really isn't any need to wash or peel them. Washing them means they steam when they cook, causing much of the flavour to disappear. It is best just to use a soft brush to gently remove any dirt.

Carpaccio is a thin shaving of raw beef or fish. Make sure raw meat is very fresh; only buy from a reputable butcher who understands this is how the meat will be consumed. Prepare and consume raw meat as soon as possible. The meat must be refrigerated at below 5°C, and should not be allowed to come to room temperature before serving.

grilled mushroom, tomato and basil salad

4 flat mushrooms (320g)
4 medium tomatoes (600g), seeded, chopped finely
2 tablespoons olive oil
2 teaspoons balsamic vinegar
2 cloves garlic, crushed
1 cup loosely packed fresh basil leaves, shredded finely
balsamic vinaigrette
¼ cup (60ml) olive oil
1 tablespoon balsamic vinegar

1 Combine mushrooms, tomato, oil, vinegar and garlic in medium bowl.
2 Cook mushrooms and tomato on heated oiled grill plate (or grill or barbecue) until browned lightly.
3 Meanwhile, make balsamic vinaigrette.
4 Divide mushrooms among serving plates; top with tomato and basil, drizzle with vinaigrette.
balsamic vinaigrette Combine ingredients in screw-top jar; shake well.
prep and cook time 20 minutes *serves* 4
nutritional count per serving 23.2g total fat (3.2g saturated fat); 1028kJ (246 cal); 3.4g carbohydrate; 4.6g protein; 4.3g fibre

beef carpaccio with thai basil salad

400g beef eye fillet, trimmed
1 cup loosely packed thai basil leaves
½ cup (40g) bean sprouts
1 fresh long red chilli, sliced thinly
chilli and peanut dressing
¼ cup (60ml) peanut oil
2 tablespoons lime juice
2 tablespoons coarsely chopped roasted unsalted peanuts
1 tablespoon japanese soy sauce
1 fresh small red thai chilli, chopped finely
1 teaspoon sesame oil
1cm piece fresh ginger (5g), grated

1 Wrap beef tightly in plastic wrap; place in freezer about 1 hour or until partially frozen. Unwrap beef; slice beef as thinly as possible to make carpaccio.
2 Make chilli and peanut dressing.
3 Combine remaining ingredients in small bowl.
4 Arrange carpaccio in single layer on serving plates; top with salad, drizzle with dressing.
chilli and peanut dressing Combine ingredients in screw-top jar; shake well.
prep time 30 minutes (+ freezing) *serves* 8
nutritional count per serving 10.8g total fat (2.4g saturated fat); 614kJ (147 cal); 0.6g carbohydrate; 11.8g protein; 0.5g fibre

sides

Achieving balance in a meal is a sure way to culinary delight. Think about how a light garden salad perfectly matches a hearty meal; an exotic mix of herbs and crisp vegetables complement a simple dish and how a classic potato salad will always get requests for seconds.

watermelon with chilli herbed salad

2 limes
½ seedless watermelon (3kg)
1 fresh long red chilli, chopped finely
½ cup finely chopped fresh coriander
¼ cup baby fresh mint leaves
½ cup baby tatsoi
lime dressing
¼ cup (60ml) lime juice
¼ cup (60ml) olive oil

1 Cut thin strips of rind from one lime then cut finely; reserve for lime dressing. Peel remaining lime; segment both limes then chop coarsely.
2 Remove and discard skin and white pith from watermelon; cut watermelon in half, then cut into eight 5cm x 8cm blocks. Cut blocks into six 1cm slices.
3 Make lime dressing.
4 Combine lime, chilli, coriander, mint and tatsoi in medium bowl.
5 Layer watermelon on large platter; sprinkle over lime and herb mixture, drizzle with dressing.
lime dressing Combine juice, oil and reserved rind in screw-top jar; shake well.
prep time 15 minutes *serves* 8
nutritional count per serving 7.4g total fat (1g saturated fat); 514kJ (123 cal); 12.4g carbohydrate; 1g protein; 1.7g fibre

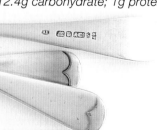

lemon and lime rice salad

2 cups (400g) basmati rice
½ cup (80g) almond kernels, chopped coarsely
¼ cup (50g) pepitas
¼ cup (35g) sunflower seed kernels
½ cup thinly sliced fresh coriander
½ cup thinly sliced fresh flat-leaf parsley
lemon and lime dressing
¼ cup (60ml) olive oil
¼ cup (60ml) lemon juice
1 teaspoon finely grated lime rind
2 tablespoons lime juice
¼ teaspoon cracked black pepper

1 Cook rice in large saucepan of boiling water, uncovered, until tender; drain. Rinse under cold water; drain. Place in large bowl.
2 Meanwhile, make lemon and lime dressing.
3 Add dressing and remaining ingredients to rice; mix gently.
lemon and lime dressing Combine ingredients in screw-top jar; shake well.
*prep and cook time 25 minutes **serves** 8*
nutritional count per serving 17.7g total fat (2.1g saturated fat); 1505kJ (360 cal); 41.6g carbohydrate; 8.1g protein; 2.4g fibre

avocado and wasabi rice salad

2 cups (400g) jasmine rice
2 medium avocados (500g), halved, chopped coarsely
2 tablespoons lime juice
1 cup (50g) snow pea tendrils, chopped coarsely
1 sheet nori, shredded finely
wasabi dressing
¾ cup (225g) mayonnaise
2 tablespoons lime juice
2 tablespoons rice wine vinegar
3 teaspoons wasabi

1 Cook rice in large saucepan of boiling water, uncovered, until tender; drain. Rinse under cold water; drain.
2 Meanwhile, make wasabi dressing.
3 Combine avocado and juice in large bowl. Add rice, dressing, tendrils and nori; mix gently.
wasabi dressing Combine ingredients in small bowl.
*prep and cook time 25 minutes **serves** 8*
nutritional count per serving 19.5g total fat (3.3g saturated fat); 1622kJ (388 cal); 47.2g carbohydrate; 5.1g protein; 1.7g fibre

olive and capsicum brown rice salad

2 cups (400g) brown rice
2 large red capsicums (700g)
1 cup (160g) fetta-stuffed green olives, sliced thinly
1 tablespoon finely chopped fresh oregano
1 fresh long red chilli, chopped finely
red wine vinaigrette
2 tablespoons lemon juice
2 tablespoons red wine vinegar
2 tablespoons olive oil
½ teaspoon white sugar
1 clove garlic, crushed

1 Cook rice in large saucepan of boiling water, uncovered, until tender; drain. Rinse under cold water; drain. Place in large bowl.
2 Meanwhile, quarter capsicums; discard seeds and membranes. Cook capsicum, skin-side up, under hot grill until skin blackens. Cover capsicum with plastic for 5 minutes; peel away skin then slice thinly.
3 Make red wine vinaigrette.
4 Add capsicum, vinaigrette and remaining ingredients to rice; mix gently.
red wine vinaigrette Combine ingredients in screw-top jar; shake well.
prep and cook time *40 minutes* **serves** *8*
nutritional count per serving *7.6g total fat (1.1g saturated fat); 1120kJ (268 cal); 42.5g carbohydrate; 5.3g protein; 4.1g fibre*

wild rice salad with spinach and figs

2 cups (400g) wild rice blend
¾ cup (90g) coarsely chopped pecans, roasted
½ cup (100g) thinly sliced dried figs
100g baby spinach leaves, chopped coarsely
2 green onions, sliced thinly
orange balsamic dressing
2 teaspoons finely grated orange rind
½ cup (125ml) orange juice
2 tablespoons olive oil
1 tablespoon white balsamic vinegar

1 Cook rice in large saucepan of boiling water, uncovered, until tender; drain. Rinse under cold water; drain. Place in large bowl.
2 Meanwhile, make orange balsamic dressing.
3 Add dressing and remaining ingredients to rice; mix gently.
orange balsamic dressing Combine ingredients in screw-top jar; shake well.
prep and cook time *15 minutes* **serves** *8*
nutritional count per serving *13g total fat (1.2g saturated fat); 1359kJ (325 cal); 44.8g carbohydrate; 5.1g protein; 3.6g fibre*

It seems a strange combination but, trust us, it's good. The salty crunch of the popcorn is great with the tang of the citrus and pomegranate and the mustard flavour of the radish. It also looks striking on the table.

pomegranate salad with chilli popcorn

¼ cup (60ml) vegetable oil
40g butter
¼ cup (60g) popping corn
1 teaspoon dried chilli flakes
¼ teaspoon sea salt flakes
4 medium oranges (1kg)
1 cup (50g) snow pea sprouts
½ cup (125ml) pomegranate pulp
6 red radishes (210g), trimmed, sliced thinly
orange dressing
¼ cup (60ml) olive oil
2 tablespoons orange juice
1 tablespoon white wine vinegar
1 teaspoon honey

You need to buy a medium pomegranate (320g) to get ½ cup pulp. To remove the pulp from the pomegranate, cut it in half, then hit the back of the fruit with a wooden spoon – the seeds usually fall out easily. Discard the shell and white pith.

1 Heat oil in medium saucepan; add butter, corn and chilli. Cook, covered, over high heat; shake pan vigorously until corn stops popping. Drain on absorbent paper; sprinkle with salt.
2 Make orange dressing.
3 Peel oranges thickly; cut crossways into 5mm slices.
4 Stack orange slices, sprouts, pomegranate and radish on serving platter; drizzle with dressing, sprinkle over popcorn.
orange dressing Combine ingredients in screw-top jar; shake well.
prep and cook time *20 minutes* **serves** *8*
nutritional count per serving *18.2g total fat (4.6g saturated fat); 1003kJ (240 cal); 14.9g carbohydrate; 2.6g protein; 4.3g fibre*

basil pesto potato salad

1kg baby new potatoes, unpeeled, quartered
½ cup (150g) mayonnaise
2 green onions, sliced thinly
¼ cup finely sliced fresh basil
2 teaspoons finely grated lemon rind
basil pesto
½ cup firmly packed fresh basil leaves
¼ cup (20g) coarsely grated parmesan cheese
2 tablespoons roasted pine nuts
1 clove garlic, quartered
⅓ cup (80ml) olive oil

1 Boil, steam or microwave potato until tender; drain.
2 Meanwhile, make basil pesto.
3 Combine mayonnaise and pesto in large bowl; add onions and hot potato, mix gently.
4 Serve salad topped with combined basil and rind.
basil pesto Process basil, cheese, nuts and garlic until chopped finely. With motor operating, gradually add oil in a thin, steady stream; process until almost smooth.
prep and cook time *30 minutes* ***serves*** *8*
nutritional count per serving *18.6g total fat (2.7g saturated fat); 1134kJ (272 cal); 20.3g carbohydrate; 4.7g protein; 3g fibre*

Buy basil pesto, instead of making your own; you'll need ½ cup.

german potato salad

1kg potatoes, unpeeled, cut into 2cm cubes
4 rindless bacon rashers (260g), sliced thinly
1 medium red onion (170g), sliced thinly
1 teaspoon black mustard seeds
⅔ cup finely chopped fresh flat-leaf parsley
sweet dijon dressing
¼ cup (60ml) cider vinegar
¼ cup (60ml) olive oil
1 tablespoon dijon mustard
½ teaspoon caster sugar

1 Boil, steam or microwave potato until tender; drain.
2 Meanwhile, make sweet dijon dressing.
3 Cook bacon in heated medium frying pan until crisp; drain on absorbent paper. Cook onion in same pan, stirring, until softened. Add mustard seeds; cook, stirring, 1 minute.
4 Combine potato, bacon, onion mixture, parsley and dressing in large bowl.
sweet dijon dressing Combine ingredients in screw-top jar; shake well.
prep and cook time *30 minutes* ***serves*** *8*
nutritional count per serving *11.3g total fat (2.6g saturated fat); 915kJ (219 cal); 18g carbohydrate; 9.8g protein; 3.1g fibre*

We used red-skinned potatoes in this recipe.

lemon, garlic and chilli potato salad

1kg baby new potatoes, unpeeled,
    cut into 1cm slices
½ cup coarsely chopped fresh flat-leaf parsley
¼ cup coarsely chopped fresh chives
lemon and chilli butter
100g butter, softened
2 cloves garlic, crushed
1 tablespoon finely grated lemon rind
1 teaspoon dried chilli flakes

1 Make lemon and chilli butter.
2 Boil, steam or microwave potato until tender; drain.
3 Combine hot potato, lemon and chilli butter, parsley and chives in large bowl.
lemon and chilli butter Combine ingredients in small bowl.
prep and cook time 30 minutes *serves* 8
nutritional count per serving 10.4g total fat (6.8g saturated fat); 744kJ (178 cal); 16.6g carbohydrate; 3.2g protein; 2.9g fibre

horseradish and tarragon potato salad

1kg large kipfler potatoes
1¼ cups (300g) sour cream
¼ cup (60ml) lemon juice
2 tablespoons prepared horseradish
2 tablespoons coarsely chopped fresh tarragon
2 stalks celery (300g), trimmed, sliced thinly
40g baby rocket leaves

1 Scrub and peel potatoes; cut lengthways into 5mm slices. Boil, steam or microwave potato until tender; drain.
2 Meanwhile, combine sour cream, juice, horseradish and tarragon in large bowl. Add celery and hot potato; toss gently to combine.
3 Serve salad topped with rocket.
prep and cook time 20 minutes *serves* 8
nutritional count per serving 15.7g total fat (10.1g saturated fat); 995kJ (238 cal); 18.8g carbohydrate; 4.3g protein; 3.1g fibre

The word burghul originally comes from the Persian word for "bruised grain". It is wheat that has been cooked and had the outer layers of bran removed and is then ground into various-sized grains. If you can't find burghul, try using couscous instead.

sumac, onion and mint salad

4 small red onions (400g), sliced thinly
2 tablespoons olive oil
2 tablespoons finely chopped fresh mint
1 tablespoon lemon juice
1 tablespoon sumac

1 Combine ingredients in medium bowl.
prep time 10 minutes *serves* 8
nutritional count per serving 4.6g total fat
(0.6g saturated fat); 238kJ (57 cal);
2.8g carbohydrate; 0.7g protein; 0.7g fibre

Any small mint leaves can be left whole, rather than chopped, if you like.

tomato & herb salad with toasted lavash

¼ cup (40g) burghul
2 tablespoons lemon juice
1 piece lavash bread (60g), cut into wedges
2 cups loosely packed fresh flat-leaf parsley leaves
1 cup coarsely chopped fresh mint
2 green onions, sliced thinly
¼ cup (60ml) olive oil
4 medium tomatoes (450g), cut into
  1cm thick slices

1 Combine burghul and juice in small bowl; refrigerate 1 hour.
2 Meanwhile, preheat oven to 180°C/160°C fan-forced.
3 Place bread on oven tray; bake about 5 minutes or until crisp.
4 Combine burghul mixture with parsley, mint, onion and oil in medium bowl.
5 Stack tomatoes with burghul mixture on serving plates; accompany with bread pieces. Drizzle extra olive oil around stack, if you like.
prep and cook time 15 minutes (+ refrigeration)
serves 4
nutritional count per serving 14.5g total fat
(2g saturated fat); 957kJ (229 cal);
17.4g carbohydrate; 4.7g protein; 5.9g fibre

four-bean salad

¼ cup (45g) dried lima beans
¼ cup (50g) dried borlotti beans
¼ cup (50g) dried kidney beans
¼ cup (50g) dried cannellini beans
125g cherry tomatoes, halved
½ small red onion (50g), sliced thinly
½ small green capsicum (75g), sliced thinly
½ cup loosely packed fresh flat-leaf parsley leaves
wholegrain mustard dressing
⅓ cup (80ml) olive oil
2 tablespoons red wine vinegar
2 teaspoons wholegrain mustard

1 Cover lima beans with cold water in medium
bowl. Cover remaining beans with cold water in
another medium bowl. Stand overnight; rinse, drain.
2 Cook beans, separately, in medium saucepans
of boiling water until tender; drain.
3 Meanwhile, make wholegrain mustard dressing.
4 Combine beans, dressing and remaining
ingredients in medium bowl.
wholegrain mustard dressing Combine
ingredients in screw-top jar; shake well.
prep and cook time *1 hour (+ standing)*
serves *8*
nutritional count per serving *9.6g total fat
(1.4g saturated fat); 681kJ (163 cal);
11.4g carbohydrate; 5.6g protein; 4.5g fibre*

mixed bean salad
with hazelnut butter

250g green beans, trimmed
250g yellow beans, trimmed
60g butter, chopped
⅓ cup (45g) finely chopped roasted hazelnuts
½ cup coarsely chopped fresh flat-leaf parsley
2 teaspoons finely grated lemon rind

1 Boil, steam or microwave beans until
tender; drain.
2 Combine warm beans with remaining
ingredients in medium bowl.
prep and cook time *15 minutes* **serves** *4*
nutritional count per serving *19.5g total fat
(8.4g saturated fat); 907kJ (217 cal);
3.8g carbohydrate; 4.7g protein; 5g fibre*

lime and coconut snake bean salad

350g snake beans, chopped coarsely
½ cup (50g) coarsely grated fresh coconut
¾ cup loosely packed fresh coriander leaves
lime and coconut dressing
¼ cup (60ml) coconut cream
1 tablespoon lime juice
2 teaspoons fish sauce
1 long green chilli, chopped finely

1 Boil, steam or microwave beans until tender; drain.
2 Meanwhile, make lime and coconut dressing.
3 Combine beans, dressing and remaining ingredients in medium bowl.
lime and coconut dressing Combine ingredients in screw-top jar; shake well.
prep and cook time *20 minutes* ***serves*** *4*
nutritional count per serving *11.5g total fat (9.9g saturated fat); 598kJ (143 cal); 3.2g carbohydrate; 4.5g protein; 4.9g fibre*

To open fresh coconut, pierce one of the eyes then roast coconut briefly in a very hot oven only until cracks appear in the shell. Cool the coconut, then break it apart and grate the flesh.

black bean and mango salad

1 cup (200g) dried black beans
1 lebanese cucumber (130g), seeded, sliced thinly
1 medium mango (430g), chopped finely
1 cup loosely packed fresh coriander leaves
sweet chilli dressing
1 tablespoon peanut oil
1 tablespoon sweet chilli sauce
1 tablespoon lime juice

1 Cover beans with cold water in medium bowl. Stand overnight; rinse, drain.
2 Cook beans in medium saucepan of boiling water until tender; drain.
3 Meanwhile, make sweet chilli dressing.
4 Combine beans, dressing and remaining ingredients in medium bowl.
sweet chilli dressing Combine ingredients in small bowl.
prep and cook time *1 hour 40 minutes (+ standing)* ***serves*** *6*
nutritional count per serving *9.9g total fat (1.5g saturated fat); 790kJ (189 cal); 9.7g carbohydrate; 11.6g protein; 7.8g fibre*

roasted mixed tomato salad

4 small red tomatoes (360g), halved
4 small green tomatoes (360g), halved
250g cherry tomatoes
200g red teardrop tomatoes
200g yellow teardrop tomatoes
2 tablespoons olive oil
2 tablespoons balsamic vinegar
2 tablespoons small fresh basil leaves
1 tablespoon fresh oregano leaves
1 tablespoon fresh thyme leaves

1 Preheat oven to 240°C/220°C fan-forced.
2 Combine tomatoes and oil in large shallow baking dish. Roast, uncovered, 10 minutes. Remove from oven; cool 30 minutes.
3 Combine tomato mixture and remaining ingredients in large bowl. Serve grissini (breadsticks) alongside salad, if you like.
prep and cook time *20 minutes (+ cooling)*
serves *10*
nutritional count per serving *3.8g total fat (0.5g saturated fat); 209kJ (50 cal); 2.4g carbohydrate; 1g protein; 1.6g fibre*

greek salad with marinated fetta

2 medium tomatoes (300g)
1 lebanese cucumber (130g)
1 small red capsicum (150g)
1 small red onion (100g), sliced thinly
1 cup (120g) seeded black olives
marinated fetta cheese
200g fetta cheese, cut into 1cm pieces
1 fresh long red chilli, chopped finely
2 teaspoons finely grated lemon rind
2 tablespoons fresh oregano leaves
1 cup (250ml) olive oil

1 Make marinated fetta cheese.
2 Halve and seed tomatoes, cucumber and capsicum; cut vegetables into matchsticks.
3 Combine a third of the marinated fetta and a third of the oil marinade with salad ingredients in large bowl.
marinated fetta cheese Place cheese in sterilised jar. Combine remaining ingredients in small jug; pour oil mixture over cheese. Refrigerate 3 hours or overnight.
prep time *25 minutes (+ refrigeration)* ***serves*** *6*
nutritional count per serving *46g total fat (10.5g saturated fat); 1969kJ (471 cal); 7.7g carbohydrate; 7.3g protein; 1.4g fibre*

Remaining marinated fetta can be stored, in the refrigerator, for up to four weeks.

curried couscous and chickpea salad

½ cup (125ml) water
½ cup (125ml) chicken stock
1 teaspoon curry powder
1 cup (200g) couscous
400g can chickpeas, rinsed, drained
200g fetta cheese, crumbled
½ cup coarsely chopped fresh coriander
2 green onions, sliced thinly
1 teaspoon finely grated lemon rind
¼ cup (60ml) lemon juice

1 Bring the water, stock and curry powder to the boil in small saucepan.
2 Combine couscous in medium heatproof bowl with stock mixture, cover; stand about 5 minutes or until water is absorbed, fluffing with fork occasionally.
3 Stir remaining ingredients into couscous.
prep and cook time *15 minutes* ***serves*** *4*
nutritional count per serving *13.6g total fat (8g saturated fat); 1701kJ (407 cal); 48.7g carbohydrate; 20.2g protein; 4g fibre*

orange and date couscous salad

1 cup (200g) couscous
1 cup (250ml) boiling water
2 medium oranges (480g)
40g baby spinach leaves
½ small red onion (50g), sliced thinly
½ cup seeded fresh dates (70g), sliced thinly
1 tablespoon olive oil

1 Combine couscous with the water in medium heatproof bowl, cover; stand about 5 minutes or until water is absorbed, fluffing with fork occasionally.
2 Meanwhile, coarsely grate rind from both oranges. Segment oranges over small bowl; reserve any juice in bowl (you need ¼ cup juice).
3 Stir orange segments, reserved juice and remaining ingredients into couscous.
prep time *15 minutes* ***serves*** *4*
nutritional count per serving *5.1g total fat (0.7g saturated fat); 1329kJ (318 cal); 56.7g carbohydrate; 8.2g protein; 4.9g fibre*

preserved lemon, mint and raisin couscous salad

1 cup (200g) couscous
1 cup (250ml) boiling water
1 teaspoon ground cumin
½ cup (75g) raisins
2 tablespoons finely chopped preserved lemon rind
1 cup coarsely chopped fresh mint
¼ cup (60ml) lemon juice

1 Combine couscous with the water in medium heatproof bowl, cover; stand about 5 minutes or until water is absorbed, fluffing with fork occasionally.
2 Stir remaining ingredients into couscous.
prep time *15 minutes* **serves** *4*
nutritional count per serving *0.7g total fat (0.1g saturated fat); 1066kJ (255 cal); 52.8g carbohydrate; 7.4g protein; 2.5g fibre*

fennel and tomato couscous salad

250g cherry tomatoes, halved
cooking-oil spray
1 cup (200g) couscous
1 cup (250ml) boiling water
2 baby fennel bulbs (260g), trimmed, sliced thinly
¼ cup (60ml) olive oil
1 tablespoon white wine vinegar
1 clove garlic, crushed
2 tablespoons finely chopped fresh oregano

1 Preheat oven to 200°C/180°C fan-forced.
2 Place tomato on oven tray; spray with cooking oil. Roast about 10 minutes or until skins burst.
3 Meanwhile, combine couscous with the water in medium heatproof bowl, cover; stand about 5 minutes or until water is absorbed, fluffing with fork occasionally.
4 Stir tomato and remaining ingredients into couscous.
prep and cook time *20 minutes* **serves** *4*
nutritional count per serving *14.8g total fat (2g saturated fat); 1384kJ (331 cal); 40.8g carbohydrate; 7.1g protein; 2.7g fibre*

Panzanella is a refreshing Tuscan summer bread salad. We've put our own spin on it by using little cubes of radish sandwich instead of the traditional bread pieces.

panzanella with radish sandwiches

4 slices white bread (180g), crusts removed
20g butter, softened
4 red radishes (140g), trimmed, sliced thinly
1 medium avocado (250g), halved, chopped coarsely
400g can butter beans, rinsed, drained
4 medium tomatoes (600g), chopped coarsely
1 medium yellow capsicum (200g), chopped coarsely
2 lebanese cucumbers (260g), chopped coarsely
1 cup firmly packed fresh basil leaves
tomato dressing
1 large tomato (220g), peeled, seeded
¼ cup (60ml) olive oil
1 tablespoon white balsamic vinegar
½ teaspoon caster sugar

To peel the tomato for the dressing, cut a shallow cross in the bottom of the tomato and put it into a bowl of just-boiled water for about 1 minute. The skin should then peel away easily. Cut the peeled tomato in half, then scoop out the seeds using a teaspoon.

1 Spread bread with butter; top two slices with radish, top with remaining bread. Using rolling pin, gently flatten radish sandwiches. Cut sandwiches into small squares.
2 Make tomato dressing.
3 Combine avocado and remaining ingredients with the dressing in large bowl. Divide salad among serving plates; top with radish sandwiches.
tomato dressing Blend or process tomato until smooth. Add remaining ingredients; pulse until combined.
prep time 30 minutes **serves** 8
nutritional count per serving *14.4g total fat (3.5g saturated fat); 8.7kJ (193 cal); 10.6g carbohydrate; 4g protein; 3.5g fibre*

semi-dried tomato tapenade pasta salad

500g large spiral pasta
250g cherry tomatoes, halved
50g baby rocket leaves
⅓ cup (25g) shaved parmesan cheese
tomato tapenade
½ cup (75g) drained semi-dried tomatoes in oil
½ cup (60g) seeded black olives
2 tablespoons olive oil
1 tablespoon red wine vinegar
2 teaspoons brown sugar

1 Cook pasta in large saucepan of boiling water until tender; drain. Rinse under cold water; drain.
2 Meanwhile, make tomato tapenade.
3 Combine pasta, tapenade and remaining ingredients in large bowl.
tomato tapenade Blend or process ingredients until smooth.
prep and cook time *20 minutes* ***serves*** *10*
nutritional count per serving *5.7g total fat (1.2g saturated fat); 1032kJ (247 cal); 39.3g carbohydrate; 7.7g protein; 3.3g fibre*

creamy tomato chutney pasta salad

500g rigatoni pasta
10 slices prosciutto (150g)
1 cup (240g) crème fraîche
½ cup (160g) tomato chutney
300g cherry bocconcini cheese, halved
1 small red onion (100g), sliced thinly
1 cup loosely packed fresh basil leaves, chopped coarsely

1 Cook pasta in large saucepan of boiling water until tender; drain. Rinse under cold water; drain.
2 Meanwhile, cook prosciutto in heated oiled large frying pan until crisp. Drain on absorbent paper; chop coarsely.
3 Combine crème fraîche and chutney in large bowl. Gently mix in pasta, prosciutto and remaining ingredients.
prep and cook time *25 minutes* ***serves*** *10*
nutritional count per serving *15.6g total fat (9.7g saturated fat); 1555kJ (372 cal); 42.3g carbohydrate; 14.3g protein; 2.2g fibre*

pasta and garlic breadcrumb salad

500g farfalle pasta
¼ cup (60ml) olive oil
100g butter, chopped
2½ cups (175g) stale breadcrumbs
4 cloves garlic, crushed
1 cup coarsely chopped fresh flat-leaf parsley

1 Cook pasta in large saucepan of boiling water until tender; drain.
2 Meanwhile, heat oil and butter in large frying pan; cook breadcrumbs and garlic over medium heat, stirring, until breadcrumbs brown.
3 Combine hot pasta, breadcrumbs and parsley in large bowl.

prep and cook time *20 minutes* ***serves*** *10*
nutritional count per serving *14.9g total fat (6.4g saturated fat); 1493kJ (357 cal); 45.8g carbohydrate; 8.2g protein; 2.9g fibre*

Farfalle is a bow-tie shaped short pasta; sometimes known as butterfly pasta.

zucchini and ricotta pasta salad

500g penne pasta
4 large zucchini (600g), sliced thinly lengthways
⅓ cup (80ml) olive oil
1 tablespoon finely grated lemon rind
⅓ cup (80ml) lemon juice
2 cloves garlic, crushed
400g ricotta cheese, crumbled
½ cup loosely packed fresh basil leaves, shredded finely

1 Cook pasta in large saucepan of boiling water until tender; drain.
2 Meanwhile, combine zucchini and half the oil in medium bowl. Cook zucchini, in batches, on heated oiled grill plate (or grill or barbecue) until tender.
3 Combine zucchini, rind, juice, garlic and remaining oil in large bowl. Gently mix in pasta, cheese and basil.

prep and cook time *25 minutes* ***serves*** *10*
nutritional count per serving *12.6g total fat (4g saturated fat); 1279kJ (306 cal); 35.g carbohydrate; 10.6g protein; 2.8g fibre*

curried egg salad

1 stalk celery (150g), trimmed,
   cut into matchsticks
¼ small red onion (25g), sliced thinly
½ cup coarsely chopped fresh flat-leaf parsley
4 hard-boiled eggs, grated finely
4 small butter lettuce leaves
curry mayonnaise
⅓ cup (100g) mayonnaise
1 tablespoon lemon juice
½ teaspoon curry powder

1 Make curry mayonnaise.
2 Combine celery, onion and parsley in medium bowl. Divide egg among lettuce leaves; top with celery mixture, drizzle with mayonnaise.
curry mayonnaise Combine ingredients in small bowl.
prep time *20 minutes* **serves** *4*
nutritional count per serving *15.2g total fat (3g saturated fat); 832kJ (199 cal); 6.1g carbohydrate; 9.3g protein; 1.2g fibre*

mixed leaf salad with cranberry dressing

1 baby cos lettuce (180g), trimmed,
   leaves separated
250g rocket, trimmed
1 small radicchio (150g), trimmed,
   leaves separated
½ cup (40g) flaked almonds, roasted
½ cup (65g) dried cranberries
cranberry dressing
¼ cup (60m) olive oil
¼ cup (60ml) red wine vinegar
2 tablespoons cranberry juice
2 teaspoons dijon mustard
1 clove garlic, crushed
2 tablespoons cranberry sauce
½ small red onion (50g), chopped finely

1 Make cranberry dressing.
2 Combine lettuce, rocket and radicchio in large serving bowl; sprinkle with nuts and cranberries, drizzle with dressing.
cranberry dressing Blend oil, vinegar, juice, mustard, garlic and sauce until combined; stir in onion.
prep time *15 minutes* **serves** *8*
nutritional count per serving *10.1g total fat (1.2g saturated fat); 619kJ (148 cal); 10.7g carbohydrate; 2.8g protein; 2.4g fibre*

winter coleslaw

2 cups (160g) finely shredded cabbage
1 baby fennel bulb (130g), trimmed, sliced thinly
100g green beans, trimmed, sliced thinly
600g celeriac, peeled, grated coarsely
1 stalk celery (150g), trimmed, sliced thinly
1 cup loosely packed fresh flat-leaf parsley leaves
cider dressing
¼ cup (60ml) olive oil
2 tablespoons cider vinegar
1 teaspoon caster sugar
1 teaspoon dijon mustard

1 Make cider dressing.
2 Combine salad ingredients and dressing in large bowl.
cider dressing Combine ingredients in screw-top jar; shake well.
prep time *25 minutes* ***serves*** *4*
nutritional count per serving *14.2g total fat (1.9g saturated fat); 941kJ (225 cal); 15.2g carbohydrate; 3.5g protein; 12.3g fibre*

We used savoy cabbage, a fairly mild-tasting cabbage, in this recipe; it has a large, heavy head with crinkled dark-green outer leaves.

asian-style coleslaw

2 cups (160g) finely shredded wombok
1 medium carrot (120g), grated coarsely
3 green onions, sliced thinly
1 cup loosely packed fresh coriander leaves
100g crispy fried noodles
plum and soy dressing
2 tablespoons peanut oil
1 tablespoon plum sauce
1 tablespoon white wine vinegar
2 teaspoons light soy sauce
1 teaspoon caster sugar

1 Make plum and soy dressing.
2 Combine salad ingredients and dressing in large bowl.
plum and soy dressing Combine ingredients in screw-top jar; shake well.
prep time *15 minutes* ***serves*** *4*
nutritional count per serving *5.6g total fat (1.1g saturated fat); 602kJ (144 cal); 18.7g carbohydrate; 3.5g protein; 2.3g fibre*

Crispy fried noodles are egg noodles that have been deep-fried then packaged for sale on supermarket shelves.

warm red cabbage and bacon salad

2 rindless bacon rashers (130g), chopped coarsely
1 tablespoon olive oil
6 cups (480g) coarsely shredded red cabbage
2 tablespoons red wine vinegar
1 tablespoon brown sugar
½ cup coarsely chopped fresh flat-leaf parsley

1 Cook bacon in heated large frying pan until crisp. Drain on absorbent paper.
2 Heat oil in same pan; cook cabbage, stirring, about 5 minutes or until softened. Add vinegar and sugar; cook, stirring, about 10 minutes or until liquid evaporates.
3 Return bacon to pan; cook, stirring, until heated through. Remove from heat; stir in parsley.
***prep and cook time** 25 minutes **serves** 4*
***nutritional count per serving** 9.2g total fat (2.2g saturated fat); 656kJ (157 cal); 7g carbohydrate; 9.1g protein; 5g fibre*

cabbage, orange and radish salad

1 medium orange (240g)
2 cups (160g) finely shredded green cabbage
2 red radishes (70g), trimmed, sliced thinly
½ cup loosely packed fresh mint leaves
cumin and orange dressing
1 teaspoon cumin seeds
¼ teaspoon hot paprika
2 tablespoons olive oil
1 tablespoon white balsamic vinegar

1 Segment orange over small bowl; reserve 1 tablespoon juice for dressing.
2 Make cumin and orange dressing.
3 Combine orange segments, dressing and remaining ingredients in large bowl.
cumin and orange dressing Dry-fry spices in heated small frying pan until fragrant; cool. Combine spices with oil, vinegar and reserved orange juice in screw-top jar; shake well.
***prep and cook time** 25 minutes **serves** 4*
***nutritional count per serving** 9.3g total fat (1.3g saturated fat); 472kJ (113 cal); 5g carbohydrate; 1.3g protein; 2.9g fibre*

mains seafood

A main-course salad can be hot, cold or warm. What sets it apart from other dishes is its amalgamation of flavours; try tuna with soba noodles or prawns with mango. It's a light, fresh, delicious way to eat.

smoked salmon, orange and avocado salad

2 large oranges (600g), segmented
2 large avocados (640g), halved, sliced thickly
2 x 150g smoked salmon portions, skinned, flaked
40g baby spinach leaves
10g lamb's lettuce
horseradish cream dressing
¼ cup (60ml) orange juice
1 tablespoon olive oil
1 tablespoon white wine vinegar
1 tablespoon horseradish cream

1 Make horseradish cream dressing.
2 Combine orange, avocado, fish, spinach and lettuce in large bowl. Divide salad among serving plates; drizzle with dressing.
horseradish cream dressing Combine ingredients in screw-top jar; shake well.
prep time *15 minutes* **serves** *4*
nutritional count per serving *35.9g total fat (7.7g saturated fat); 1856kJ (444 cal); 10.9g carbohydrate; 18.3g protein; 4.3g fibre*

You need about two punnets of lamb's lettuce for this recipe.
You can use smoked ocean trout portions instead of the salmon, if you like.

salmon and pickled ginger salad

100g rice vermicelli
800g salmon fillets, skin on
3 shallots (75g), sliced thinly
1 cup loosely packed fresh coriander leaves
2 tablespoons drained pickled ginger in syrup, sliced finely
sesame soy dressing
1 tablespoon sesame seeds, toasted
2 tablespoons lemon juice
1 tablespoon pickled ginger syrup (see note, left)
1 tablespoon light soy sauce
1 tablespoon kecap manis
2 teaspoons sesame oil
2 teaspoons olive oil

For the pickled ginger syrup in the dressing, use the syrup drained from the pickled ginger in the salad. The salmon skin gets wonderfully crunchy when cooked twice on the grill, as we do in this recipe; this provides added texture and flavour to the salad.

1 Place vermicelli in large heatproof bowl; cover with boiling water. Stand until just tender; drain. Rinse under cold water; drain.
2 Meanwhile, cook fish, skin-side down, on heated oiled grill plate (or grill or barbecue) about 5 minutes or until skin is crisp. Turn fish; cook about 4 minutes or until cooked as desired. Lift skin from fish; cook skin, on same grill plate, until crisp. Slice skin finely; flake fish into large pieces.
3 Make sesame soy dressing.
4 Combine vermicelli, shallot, coriander, ginger and half the dressing in large bowl; divide among serving plates. Top with fish, drizzle with remaining dressing; sprinkle with crisp salmon skin.
sesame soy dressing Combine ingredients in small bowl.
prep and cook time *35 minutes* ***serves*** *4*
nutritional count per serving *20.7g total fat (4g saturated fat); 1793kJ (429 cal); 17.7g carbohydrate; 42.3g protein; 1.3g fibre*

tuna and soba salad with coriander dressing

270g soba noodles

700g tuna steaks

1 lebanese cucumber (130g), seeded, sliced thinly

2 green onions, sliced thinly

1 sheet nori, shredded finely

1 tablespoon black cumin seeds

coriander dressing

½ cup firmly packed fresh coriander leaves

¼ cup (60ml) light olive oil

¼ cup (60ml) lemon juice

2 tablespoons rice wine vinegar

1 teaspoon sesame oil

1cm piece fresh ginger (5g), grated

1 clove garlic, quartered

1 Cook noodles in large saucepan of boiling water until tender; drain. Rinse under cold water; drain.

2 Meanwhile, make coriander dressing.

3 Cook fish on heated oiled grill plate (or grill or barbecue) until cooked as desired. Slice fish thickly.

4 Combine noodles, cucumber, onion, nori, seeds and dressing in large bowl. Divide salad among serving plates; top with fish.

coriander dressing Blend or process ingredients until combined.

*prep and cook time 30 minutes **serves** 6*
nutritional count per serving 17.1g total fat
(4.2g saturated fat); 1781kJ (426 cal);
31.8g carbohydrate; 34.8g protein; 2.3g fibre

tuna potato salad

2 medium potatoes (400g), unpeeled,
   sliced thickly

1 tablespoon olive oil

20g butter

200g green beans, trimmed

500g tuna steaks

1 large tomato (220g), cut into wedges

⅔ cup (80g) seeded black olives

¼ cup loosely packed fresh mint leaves

lemon dressing

⅓ cup (80ml) lemon juice

2 tablespoons olive oil

1 clove garlic, crushed

½ teaspoon ground cumin

1 Boil, steam or microwave potato until tender; drain.

2 Heat oil and butter in medium frying pan; cook potato, in batches, until browned lightly. Drain on absorbent paper.

3 Meanwhile, boil, steam or microwave beans until tender; drain. Rinse under cold water; drain.

4 Make lemon dressing.

5 Cook fish on heated oiled grill plate (or grill or barbecue) until cooked as desired. Slice fish thinly.

6 Divide potato, beans, tomato and olives among serving plates; top with fish, drizzle with dressing then sprinkle with mint.

lemon dressing Combine ingredients in screw-top jar; shake well.

*prep and cook time 35 minutes **serves** 4*
nutritional count per serving 25.4g total fat
(7.6g saturated fat); 1935kJ (463 cal);
20.6g carbohydrate; 38.9g protein; 4.6g fibre

We leave the tails on the prawns so they keep their shape and look good. You can turn this dish into easy-eating fork food by removing the tails when shelling the prawns.

mango and prawn salad

1kg uncooked medium king prawns
2 tablespoons light soy sauce
2 teaspoons sesame oil
1 fresh long red chilli, chopped finely
2 teaspoons finely chopped fresh coriander root and stem mixture
1cm piece fresh ginger (5g), grated
2 cloves garlic, crushed
1 medium mango (430g), sliced thinly
1 large red capsicum (350g), sliced thinly
1 lebanese cucumber (130g), seeded, sliced thinly
1 cup (80g) bean sprouts
½ cup loosely packed fresh coriander leaves
2 green onions, sliced thinly
lime dressing
⅓ cup (80ml) lime juice
1 tablespoon grated palm sugar
2 teaspoons fish sauce

1 Shell and devein prawns, leaving tails intact. Combine prawns in medium bowl with sauce, oil, chilli, root and stem mixture, ginger and garlic. Refrigerate 30 minutes.
2 Meanwhile, make lime dressing.
3 Cook prawns in heated large frying pan, in batches, until changed in colour.
4 Combine prawns, dressing and remaining ingredients in large bowl.
lime dressing Combine ingredients in screw-top jar; shake well.
prep and cook time *35 minutes (+ refrigeration)* ***serves*** *4*
nutritional count per serving *3.5g total fat (0.5g saturated fat); 970kJ (232 cal); 18g carbohydrate; 29.7g protein; 3.6g fibre*

beetroot and fennel salad
with caraway salmon

1 small fennel bulb (200g), trimmed
1 medium beetroot (175g), peeled
1 small radicchio (150g), trimmed, shredded finely
½ cup loosely packed fresh flat-leaf parsley leaves
1 tablespoon rice wine vinegar
¼ cup (60ml) olive oil
4 salmon fillets (880g)
1½ teaspoons caraway seeds
1 clove garlic, crushed
1 lime, cut into wedges

1 Using mandolin, V-slicer or very sharp knife, slice fennel and beetroot finely. Place in large bowl with radicchio, parsley, vinegar and 2 tablespoons of the oil.
2 Combine fish, remaining oil, seeds and garlic in large bowl. Cook fish in heated large frying pan until cooked as desired.
3 Divide salad and fish among serving plates; serve with lime.
prep and cook time 30 minutes **serves** 4
nutritional count per serving 29.5g total fat (5.5g saturated fat); 1960kJ (469 cal); 4.8g carbohydrate; 44.7g protein; 3.6g fibre

garlic prawns and tatsoi salad

4 x 9cm-square wonton wrappers
1kg uncooked medium king prawns
4 cloves garlic, crushed
2 teaspoons olive oil
80g tatsoi leaves
1 fresh long red chilli, cut into matchsticks
ginger soy dressing
¼ cup (60ml) peanut oil
1 teaspoon sesame oil
2 tablespoons lime juice
1 tablespoon light soy sauce
1cm piece fresh ginger (5g), grated

1 Preheat oven to 200°C/180°C fan-forced. Grease and line two oven trays.
2 Place wonton wrappers on trays; bake about 5 minutes or until crisp.
3 Make ginger soy dressing
4 Shell and devein prawns, leaving tails intact; combine prawns and garlic in medium bowl. Heat oil in large frying pan; cook prawns until changed in colour.
5 Combine tatsoi, chilli and half the dressing in large bowl.
6 Divide salad among serving plates; top with prawns, drizzle with remaining dressing. Serve with wontons.
ginger soy dressing Combine ingredients in screw-top jar; shake well.
prep and cook 30 minutes **serves** 4
nutritional count per serving 18.1g total fat (3.1g saturated fat); 1208kJ (289 cal); 4g carbohydrate; 27g protein; 1.2g fibre

Poaching is a great low-fat way to cook fish because you don't need to use oil. You'll have very tender flesh, lightly infused with the flavours of the poaching liquid. Ensure the liquid is only just simmering, as slow cooking provides the most delicate flesh.

poached trout and potato salad

800g kipfler potatoes, unpeeled, halved
1 litre (4 cups) water
4 x 5cm strips lemon rind
2 sprigs fresh dill
600g ocean trout fillets
1 small red onion (100g), sliced thinly
1 lebanese cucumber (130g), seeded, sliced thinly
50g rocket leaves
lemon and dill dressing
⅓ cup (80ml) olive oil
¼ cup (60ml) lemon juice
1 clove garlic, crushed
1 tablespoon finely chopped fresh dill
1 tablespoon rinsed, drained baby capers

1 Boil, steam or microwave potato until tender; drain.
2 Combine the water, rind and dill in medium saucepan; bring to the boil. Add fish; simmer, covered, about 10 minutes or until cooked as desired. Drain fish; discard cooking liquid. Flake fish coarsely into large bowl; discard skin.
3 Meanwhile, make lemon and dill dressing.
4 Add potato, dressing and remaining ingredients to bowl with fish; toss gently to combine.
lemon and dill dressing Combine ingredients in screw-top jar; shake well.
prep and cook time *25 minutes* **serves** *4*
nutritional count per serving *24.3g total fat (3.9g saturated fat); 2031kJ (486 cal); 29.3g carbohydrate; 34.9g protein; 5.1g fibre*

crispy whitebait salad with garlic mayonnaise

2 tablespoons salt

2 tablespoons dried chilli flakes

1 tablespoon sweet paprika

¾ cup (135g) semolina

1 cup (170g) polenta

500g whitebait

vegetable oil, for deep-frying

1 lebanese cucumber (130g),
   cut into matchsticks

1 medium red capsicum (200g),
   cut into matchsticks

1 small red onion (100g), sliced thinly

80g mizuna

garlic mayonnaise

½ cup (150g) mayonnaise

4 cloves garlic, crushed

2 tablespoons lemon juice

1 Make garlic mayonnaise.

2 Combine salt, chilli, paprika, semolina and polenta in large bowl, add whitebait; toss fish to coat in mixture.

3 Heat oil in wok; deep-fry fish, in batches, until browned lightly. Drain on absorbent paper.

4 Combine remaining ingredients in large bowl; divide salad among serving plates. Top with fish; serve with mayonnaise.

garlic mayonnaise Combine ingredients in small bowl.

prep and cook 40 minutes **serves** *4*

nutritional count per serving *35.1g total fat (6.1g saturated fat); 2964kJ (709 cal); 64g carbohydrate; 31.8g protein; 4.8g fibre*

warm squid and tomato salad

1 cup (120g) seeded black olives,
   chopped coarsely

400g fetta cheese, crumbled

1 tablespoon finely grated lemon rind

½ cup loosely packed fresh oregano leaves

12 cleaned small squid hoods (700g)

4 medium egg tomatoes (300g), quartered

1 large red onion (300g), cut into wedges

2 tablespoons olive oil

1 baby endive (300g), trimmed

oregano and red wine dressing

¼ cup (60ml) olive oil

2 tablespoons red wine vinegar

1 clove garlic, crushed

1 tablespoon finely chopped fresh oregano

1 Preheat oven to 180°C/160°C fan-forced.

2 Combine olives, cheese, rind and oregano in small bowl; push cheese mixture into squid hoods. Secure with toothpicks; refrigerate until required.

3 Place tomato and onion in large baking dish; drizzle with oil. Roast about 15 minutes or until tomato begins to soften. Remove dish from oven. Place squid on top of tomato mixture. Roast about 10 minutes or until squid are cooked through.

4 Meanwhile, make oregano and red wine dressing.

5 Combine tomato, onion and endive in large bowl; divide salad among serving plates. Top with squid; drizzle with dressing.

oregano and red wine dressing Combine ingredients in screw-top jar; shake well.

prep and cook time 45 minutes **serves** *4*

nutritional count per serving *48.8g total fat (19.3g saturated fat); 2913kJ (697 cal); 13.2g carbohydrate; 50.2g protein; 4.3g fibre*

Palm sugar is made from the sap of palm trees, which is then boiled down to a hard consistency; it is bought in block form. It has a distinctive caramel taste, and is often used in Asian recipes to balance sour or spicy flavours. It is available in supermarkets and Asian grocery stores, however, you can use brown sugar in its place if you prefer.

tamarind and chilli octopus salad

1kg cleaned baby octopus
1 tablespoon tamarind concentrate
1 fresh small red thai chilli, chopped finely
2 tablespoons peanut oil
1 cup (80g) bean sprouts
1 cup (50g) snow pea sprouts
100g snow peas, trimmed,
   sliced thinly lengthways
1 small red capsicum (150g), sliced thinly
1 cup loosely packed fresh coriander leaves
lime and palm sugar dressing
¼ cup (60ml) peanut oil
1 teaspoon finely grated lime rind
2 tablespoons lime juice
1 tablespoon grated palm sugar

1 Make lime and palm sugar dressing.
2 Combine octopus, tamarind, chilli and half the oil in large bowl.
3 Heat remaining oil in wok; stir-fry octopus, in batches, until cooked.
4 Combine octopus, dressing and remaining ingredients in large bowl.
lime and palm sugar dressing Combine ingredients in screw-top jar; shake well.
prep and cook time *35 minutes* ***serves*** *4*
nutritional count per serving *24.7g total fat (4.1g saturated fat); 1806kJ (432 cal); 7.6g carbohydrate; 43.9g protein; 2.5g fibre*

grilled balmain bug salad

2 baby eggplants (120g)
1 medium zucchini (120g)
1 medium red capsicum (200g), chopped finely
3 flat mushrooms (240g), quartered
2 tablespoons olive oil
6 uncooked balmain bug tails (1.5kg),
   halved lengthways
250g rocket, trimmed
chilli lime butter
60g butter, softened
2 teaspoons finely grated lime rind
2 tablespoons lime juice
1 fresh long red chilli, chopped finely
2 cloves garlic, crushed

1 Using vegetable peeler, cut eggplant and zucchini into long, thin strips. Combine eggplant, zucchini, capsicum, mushrooms and oil in large bowl.
2 Cook vegetables, in batches, on heated oiled grill plate (or grill or barbecue) until tender. Cover to keep warm.
3 Cook balmain bug on heated oiled grill plate until cooked.
4 Meanwhile, make chilli lime butter.
5 Combine vegetables, balmain bug and chilli lime butter in large bowl.
6 Divide rocket among serving plates; top with vegetable and balmain bug mixture.
chilli lime butter Combine ingredients in small bowl.
prep and cook time *40 minutes* ***serves*** *4*
nutritional count per serving *25.1g total fat (10g saturated fat); 2282kJ (456 cal); 5.4g carbohydrate; 72.4g protein; 4.6g fibre*

Prawns or crabs can be used instead of balmain bugs.

mains poultry

cajun chicken caesar salad

½ small french bread stick (75g)
20g butter, melted
1 tablespoon finely chopped fresh flat-leaf parsley
2 tablespoons olive oil
4 slices prosciutto (60g)
600g chicken breast fillets
2 teaspoons cajun spice mix
1 baby cos lettuce (180g), leaves separated
½ cup (40g) shaved parmesan cheese
caesar dressing
1 egg
1 clove garlic, quartered
2 tablespoons lemon juice
½ teaspoon dijon mustard
5 drained anchovy fillets
⅔ cup (160ml) olive oil

1 Preheat oven to 200°C/180°C fan-forced.
2 Break bread into pieces; combine bread, butter, parsley and half the oil in medium bowl. Place bread pieces, in single layer, on oiled oven tray; toast about 10 minutes.
3 Meanwhile, make caesar dressing.
4 Cook prosciutto in heated large frying pan until crisp. Drain on absorbent paper; cool. Break prosciutto into pieces.
5 Combine chicken, spice mix and remaining oil in medium bowl; cook chicken in same heated pan until cooked. Cover chicken; stand 5 minutes then shred coarsely.
6 Combine chicken, prosciutto, toast and remaining ingredients in large bowl. Drizzle with dressing.
caesar dressing Blend or process egg, garlic, juice, mustard and anchovy until smooth. With motor operating, add oil in a thin steady stream; process until dressing thickens slightly.
prep and cook time *45 minutes* ***serves*** *4*
nutritional count per serving *63.1g total fat (14.2g saturated fat); 3277kJ (784 cal); 11g carbohydrate; 43.8g protein; 1.8g fibre*

sesame chicken with honey soy dressing

600g chicken breast fillets, halved lengthways
1 egg white, beaten lightly
½ cup (75g) sesame seeds
2 tablespoons olive oil
100g asian greens
1 small red onion (100g), sliced thinly
⅔ cup (100g) coarsely chopped roasted
   unsalted cashew nuts
honey soy dressing
¼ cup (60ml) lemon juice
2 tablespoons light soy sauce
1 tablespoon olive oil
2 teaspoons honey
½ teaspoon sesame oil

1 Dip chicken in egg white, then coat in sesame seeds. Heat oil in large frying pan; cook chicken until cooked through. Cover chicken; stand 5 minutes then slice thickly.
2 Meanwhile, make honey soy dressing.
3 Place greens, onion and nuts on serving plates; top with chicken, drizzle with dressing.
honey soy dressing Combine ingredients in small bowl.
prep and cook time 25 minutes **serves** *4*
nutritional count per serving 45.9g total fat (8g saturated fat); 2638kJ (631 cal); 11.8g carbohydrate; 42.1g protein; 3.8g fibre

crispy duck and fig salad with spiced balsamic glaze

600g duck breast fillets, skin on
80g trimmed watercress
250g yellow grape tomatoes, halved
4 medium figs (240g), cut into wedges
spiced balsamic glaze
½ cup (125ml) balsamic vinegar
2 tablespoons brown sugar
½ teaspoon ground cinnamon
¼ teaspoon ground clove

1 Make spiced balsamic glaze.
2 Meanwhile, cook duck, skin-side down, in heated oiled large frying pan about 5 minutes or until skin is crisp. Turn duck; cook about 5 minutes or until cooked as desired. Cover, stand 5 minutes then slice duck thinly.
3 Place watercress and tomato in medium bowl with dressing; toss gently. Divide figs among plates; top with tomato mixture then duck.
spiced balsamic glaze Combine ingredients in small saucepan; stir over low heat, without boiling, until sugar dissolves. Bring to the boil; reduce heat. Simmer, uncovered, about 5 minutes or until syrup thickens slightly. Cool. If glaze becomes too thick, stir in a little boiling water.
prep and cook time 25 minutes **serves** *4*
nutritional count per serving 55.6g total fat (16.7g saturated fat); 2650kJ (634 cal); 12.6g carbohydrate; 21g protein; 2.9g fibre

smoked chicken, spinach and almond salad

350g smoked chicken breast fillets, sliced thinly
3 stalks celery (450g), trimmed, sliced thinly
3 small tomatoes (270g), quartered, seeded
100g baby spinach leaves
4 hard-boiled eggs, quartered
2 green onions, sliced thinly
½ cup (70g) slivered almonds, roasted
cumin mayonnaise
2 teaspoons cumin seeds, toasted
½ cup (150g) mayonnaise
¼ cup (60ml) lemon juice

1 Make cumin mayonnaise.
2 Combine chicken, celery, tomato, spinach, egg, onion and nuts in large bowl.
3 Divide salad among serving plates; drizzle over mayonnaise.
cumin mayonnaise Using mortar and pestle, crush seeds finely; combine with mayonnaise and juice in small bowl.

prep and cook time 30 minutes **serves** 4
nutritional count per serving 33.5g total fat (5.3g saturated fat); 2044kJ (489 cal); 11.3g carbohydrate; 34g protein; 4.7g fibre

smoked chicken, peach and pecan salad

170g asparagus, trimmed, cut into 3cm lengths
600g smoked chicken breast fillets, sliced thinly
1 small red onion (100g), sliced thinly
2 medium peaches (300g), sliced thinly
1 cup (120g) roasted pecans
150g baby spinach leaves
dill vinaigrette
⅓ cup (80ml) olive oil
2 tablespoons cider vinegar
1 tablespoon finely chopped fresh dill

1 Boil, steam or microwave asparagus until tender; drain. Rinse under cold water; drain.
2 Make dill vinaigrette.
3 Combine asparagus and vinaigrette with remaining ingredients in large bowl.
dill vinaigrette Combine ingredients in screw-top jar; shake well.

prep and cook time 20 minutes **serves** 4
nutritional count per serving 50.5g total fat (6.9g saturated fat); 2750kJ (658 cal); 7.4g carbohydrate; 42.4g protein; 5.2g fibre

warm duck, apple and walnut salad

2 large Granny Smith apples (400g) unpeeled, quartered, cored
¾ cup (180ml) cider vinegar
¾ cup (180ml) water
1 tablespoon brown sugar
2 x 5cm strips lemon rind
1 cinnamon stick
1 star anise
4 duck breast fillets (600g), skin on
1 teaspoon sea salt flakes
1 teaspoon ground sichuan pepper
¼ teaspoon ground ginger
40g butter
80g baby spinach leaves
4 green onions, cut into 3cm pieces
¼ cup (25g) coarsely chopped walnuts
sweet mustard dressing
2 tablespoons rice vinegar
1 tablespoon olive oil
2 teaspoons mirin
1 teaspoon dijon mustard

Refrigerating the apples after they have been cooked, helps them to hold their shape.

1 Combine apple, vinegar, the water, sugar, rind, cinnamon and star anise in medium saucepan; bring to the boil. Reduce heat; simmer, uncovered, about 8 minutes or until apple is tender. Drain; gently cut each apple in half lengthways. Refrigerate 20 minutes.

2 Meanwhile, make sweet mustard dressing.

3 Remove excess fat from duck; rub duck with combined salt, pepper and ginger. Prick duck skins with fork several times. Cook duck, skin-side down, in heated oiled large frying pan about 8 minutes or until crisp. Turn duck; cook about 5 minutes or until cooked as desired. Cover duck; stand 5 minutes then slice thinly.

4 Meanwhile, heat butter in medium frying pan; cook apple, turning occasionally, until caramelised.

5 Divide combined spinach and onion among serving plates; top with duck, apple and nuts, drizzle with dressing.

sweet mustard dressing Combine ingredients in screw-top jar; shake well.

prep and cook time 45 minutes (+ refrigeration) **serves** 4
nutritional count per serving 72.6g total fat (23g saturated fat); 3290kJ (787 cal); 12.6g carbohydrate; 21.5g protein; 2.7g fibre

Preserved lemon has a very strong sour flavour. Trim the pieces so you only use the lemon peel and none of the pulp. Wild rice blend is a mixture of white long-grain rice and the dark brown seed of a North American aquatic grass. It has a nutty flavour and crunchy texture. You'll need ¾ cup (150g) of uncooked wild rice blend for the required amount of cooked rice.

chicken and kumara salad with maple dressing

2 teaspoons mixed spice
800g chicken breast fillets
1 medium kumara (400g), sliced thinly
1 large red onion (300g), cut into wedges
100g baby rocket leaves
maple dressing
¼ cup (60ml) olive oil
2 tablespoons malt vinegar
2 tablespoons orange juice
1 tablespoon maple syrup
2 teaspoons dijon mustard

1 Make maple dressing.
2 Rub mixed spice all over chicken; cook chicken on heated oiled grill plate (or grill or barbecue) until cooked. Cover chicken; stand 5 minutes then slice thinly.
3 Meanwhile, cook kumara and onion on heated oiled grill plate until tender.
4 Combine chicken, kumara, onion and rocket in large bowl with dressing.
maple dressing Combine ingredients in screw-top jar; shake well.
prep and cook time *40 minutes* ***serves*** *4*
nutritional count per serving *25g total fat (5.3g saturated fat); 2107kJ (504 cal); 21.9g carbohydrate; 46.3g protein; 3g fibre*

chicken, preserved lemon and cranberry rice salad

2 cups (500ml) water
4 x 5cm strips lemon rind
600g chicken breast fillets
3 cups cooked wild rice blend
1 cup thinly sliced fresh mint
½ cup (65g) dried cranberries
2 tablespoons finely chopped
   preserved lemon rind
lemon cranberry dressing
⅓ cup (80ml) olive oil
¼ cup (60ml) cranberry juice
2 tablespoons lemon juice
2 teaspoons caster sugar
1 tablespoon cranberry sauce

1 Combine the water and rind in medium saucepan; bring to the boil. Add chicken; reduce heat. Simmer, covered, about 10 minutes or until chicken is cooked through. Cool chicken in liquid 10 minutes; drain. Slice chicken thinly.
2 Meanwhile, make lemon cranberry dressing.
3 Combine chicken, dressing and remaining ingredients in large bowl.
lemon cranberry dressing Combine ingredients in screw-top jar; shake well.
prep and cook time *25 minutes* ***serves*** *4*
nutritional count per serving *27.1g total fat (5.2g saturated fat); 2646kJ (633 cal); 59.3g carbohydrate; 36.3g protein; 3.2g fibre*

barbecued duck and lychee salad

1kg chinese barbecued duck
565g can lychees in syrup, drained, halved
6 trimmed red radishes (90g), sliced thinly
60g mizuna, torn
½ cup coarsely chopped fresh mint leaves
2 green onions, sliced thinly
kaffir lime and chilli dressing
¼ cup (60m) lime juice
1 tablespoon olive oil
1 teaspoon fish sauce
1 teaspoon grated palm sugar
2 fresh kaffir lime leaves, sliced thinly
1 fresh small red thai chilli, chopped finely
1 clove garlic, crushed

1 Remove skin and meat from duck; discard bones. Slice skin thickly and meat thinly.
2 Make kaffir lime and chilli dressing.
3 Combine duck, dressing and remaining ingredients in large bowl.
kaffir lime and chilli dressing Combine ingredients in screw-top jar; shake well.
prep time *25 minutes* ***serves*** *4*
nutritional count per serving *41.9g total fat (11.8g saturated fat); 2416kJ (578 cal); 20.3g carbohydrate; 29.6g protein; 2.7g fibre*

quail with radicchio and pear salad

4 quails (640g)
16 fresh sage leaves
4 slices prosciutto (60g), halved lengthways
2 teaspoons olive oil
1 ruby red grapefruit (350g)
40g butter
2 small pears (360g), cut into wedges
2 small radicchio (300g), trimmed,
    leaves separated
balsamic dressing
2 tablespoons balsamic vinegar
1 tablespoon olive oil
1 clove garlic, crushed

1 Using kitchen scissors, cut along sides of each quail's backbone; discard backbones. Halve each quail along breastbone. Place 2 sage leaves on each quail half; wrap with slice of prosciutto.
2 Heat oil in large frying pan; cook quail, in batches, about 10 minutes or until cooked.
3 Meanwhile, segment grapefruit over small bowl; reserve 1 tablespoon of juice for dressing.
4 Make balsamic dressing.
5 Heat butter in medium frying pan; add pear, cook about 4 minutes or until tender.
6 Divide radicchio, grapefruit and pear among serving plates; top with quail, drizzle with dressing.
balsamic dressing Combine vinegar, oil, garlic and reserved grapefruit juice in screw-top jar; shake well.
prep and cook time *45 minutes* ***serves*** *4*
nutritional count per serving *25.1g total fat (9g saturated fat); 1522kJ (364 cal); 13.6g carbohydrate; 19.4g protein; 3.9g fibre*

Drain the morello sour
cherries and reserve the
syrup for use in the recipe.

turkey larb with sour cherries

1 tablespoon peanut oil
600g turkey mince
2 cloves garlic, crushed
2cm piece fresh ginger (10g), grated
1 fresh long red chilli, chopped finely
2 tablespoons brown sugar
1 tablespoon fish sauce
1 tablespoon japanese soy sauce
2 tablespoons morello sour cherry syrup
1 cup (200g) drained seeded morello sour cherries
1 cup loosely packed fresh coriander leaves
8 medium cos lettuce leaves
½ cup (40g) bean sprouts

1 Heat oil in wok; stir-fry mince, garlic, ginger and chilli until mince changes colour. Remove from wok.
2 Add sugar, sauces and cherry syrup; bring to the boil. Reduce heat; simmer, uncovered, 2 minutes. Return turkey mixture to wok; cook, uncovered, about 2 minutes or until larb mixture is slightly dry and sticky. Add cherries; stir until hot. Remove from heat; stir in coriander.
3 Divide larb mixture among lettuce leaves; sprinkle with sprouts.
prep and cook time 30 minutes **serves** 4
nutritional count per serving 16.7g total fat (4.5g saturated fat); 1618kJ (387 cal); 26.7g carbohydrate; 30.9g protein; 2g fibre

chicken and rocket pesto pasta salad

375g large shell pasta
1 cup (120g) frozen peas
3 cups (480g) shredded barbecued chicken
40g baby rocket leaves
rocket pesto
40g baby rocket leaves
2 tablespoons pine nuts, roasted
½ cup (40g) finely grated parmesan cheese
2 teaspoons finely grated lemon rind
1 tablespoon lemon juice
¼ cup (60ml) olive oil

1 Cook pasta in large saucepan of boiling water until tender. Add peas during last 2 minutes of pasta cooking time; drain.
2 Meanwhile, make rocket pesto.
3 Combine pasta, peas and rocket pesto in large bowl with remaining ingredients.
rocket pesto Blend or process rocket, nuts, cheese, rind and juice until finely chopped. With motor operating, gradually add oil in a thin steady stream; blend until pesto is smooth.
prep and cook time 30 minutes **serves** 4
nutritional count per serving 32.4g total fat (7.1g saturated fat); 3168kJ (758 cal); 66.6g carbohydrate; 47g protein; 5.6g fibre

You need one large barbecued chicken, weighing approximately 900g, for this recipe.

mains beef & veal

thai beef salad with chilli and lime

500g beef fillet, trimmed

100g rice vermicelli

1 lebanese cucumber (130g), seeded, sliced thinly

½ cup firmly packed fresh coriander leaves

⅓ cup firmly packed fresh thai basil leaves

10cm stick lemon grass (20g), crushed, sliced thinly

2 fresh kaffir lime leaves, shredded finely

2 shallots (50g), sliced thinly

2 tablespoons fried shallots

thai dressing

2 fresh small red thai chillies, halved

1 clove garlic, quartered

¼ teaspoon caster sugar

⅓ cup (80ml) lime juice

2 tablespoons fish sauce

1 Cook beef on heated oiled grill plate (or grill or barbecue) until cooked as desired. Cover beef; stand 5 minutes then slice thinly.

2 Meanwhile, place vermicelli in medium heatproof bowl, cover with boiling water; stand until tender, drain. Rinse under cold water; drain.

3 Make thai dressing.

4 Combine beef, vermicelli, cucumber, herbs, lemon grass, lime leaves and sliced shallot in large bowl. Divide salad among serving plates; drizzle with dressing, sprinkle with fried shallots.

thai dressing Using mortar and pestle, crush chilli, garlic and sugar to a paste. Combine paste with remaining ingredients in small bowl.

prep and cook time *30 minutes* ***serves*** *4*
nutritional count per serving *8.3g total fat (3.2g saturated fat); 1133kJ (271 cal); 18.6g carbohydrate; 29.5g protein; 1.5g fibre*

Fried shallots can be bought in jars from Asian grocery stores.

Tortiglioni is a tubular pasta that's often served with thick sauces or in casseroles. You could use rigatoni or penne pasta instead of the tortiglioni. Any leftover bolognese sauce can be used to make this pasta salad.

blackened steak salad

2 pocket pitta breads (170g)
500g beef fillet
2 teaspoons hot paprika
1 teaspoon ground black pepper
½ teaspoon cayenne pepper
¼ teaspoon dried oregano
¼ teaspoon dried thyme
3 medium tomatoes (450g), chopped finely
1 large green capsicum (350g), chopped finely
1 lebanese cucumber (130g), seeded,
    chopped finely
½ cup coarsely chopped fresh mint
1 tablespoon olive oil
1 tablespoon balsamic vinegar
1 clove garlic, crushed

1 Preheat grill to hot.
2 Split breads in half; grill both sides until browned lightly. Break into coarse pieces.
3 Rub beef with combined spices; cook on heated oiled grill plate (or grill or barbecue) until cooked as desired. Cover beef; stand 5 minutes then slice thinly.
4 Meanwhile, combine remaining ingredients in large bowl. Arrange beef on serving plates; top with salad. Serve with bread.
*prep and cook time 30 minutes **serves** 4*
nutritional count per serving 13.3g total fat (3.9g saturated fat); 1542kJ (369 cal); 26.8g carbohydrate; 32.9g protein; 4.1g fibre

warm creamy bolognese pasta salad

1 tablespoon olive oil
1 medium brown onion (150g), chopped finely
1 medium carrot (120g), chopped finely
1 stalk celery (150g), trimmed, chopped finely
500g beef mince
1 cup (250ml) milk
30g butter
1 cup (250ml) beef stock
1 cup (260g) bottled tomato pasta sauce
½ cup (125ml) dry red wine
2 tablespoons tomato paste
2 tablespoons coarsely chopped fresh
    flat-leaf parsley
375g tortiglioni pasta
½ cup (75g) drained semi-dried tomatoes in oil,
    chopped coarsely
80g baby spinach leaves
4 green onions, sliced thinly

1 Heat oil in large saucepan; cook brown onion, carrot and celery, stirring, until carrot softens. Add mince; cook, stirring, until mince changes colour. Stir in milk and butter; cook, stirring occasionally, until liquid reduces by half. Add stock, pasta sauce, wine and paste; simmer, uncovered, about 1 hour or until sauce thickens. Remove from heat; stir in parsley. Cool 20 minutes.
2 Meanwhile, cook pasta in large saucepan of boiling water until tender; drain. Rinse under cold water; drain.
3 Combine pasta in large bowl with chopped tomato, spinach, green onion and beef mixture.
prep and cook time 1 hour 15 minutes (+ cooling)
serves 6
nutritional count per serving 5.6g total fat (2.4g saturated fat); 610kJ (146 cal); 15.2g carbohydrate; 7.9g protein; 1.8g fibre

vietnamese marinated beef salad

400g beef fillet, sliced thinly
2 teaspoons finely grated lime rind
¼ cup (60ml) lime juice
1 tablespoon fish sauce
1 tablespoon grated palm sugar
1 clove garlic, crushed
10cm stick lemon grass (20g), crushed,
    chopped finely
1 fresh small red thai chilli, chopped finely
2cm piece fresh ginger (10g), grated
¼ cup (60ml) peanut oil
1 cup (80g) bean sprouts
1 medium red capsicum (200g), sliced thinly
1 medium carrot (120g), cut into matchsticks
1 cup loosely packed vietnamese mint leaves
1 cup loosely packed fresh coriander leaves

1 Combine beef, rind, juice, sauce, sugar, garlic, lemon grass, chilli, ginger and 2 tablespoons of the oil in medium bowl; refrigerate 1 hour.
2 Heat remaining oil in wok; stir-fry beef mixture, in batches, until browned.
3 Combine beef with remaining ingredients in large bowl.

prep and cook time 25 minutes (+ refrigeration)
serves 4

nutritional count per serving 20g total fat
(5g saturated fat); 1325kJ (317 cal);
8.7g carbohydrate; 24.1g protein; 3.6g fibre

grilled veal and radicchio salad

600g veal fillet
1 tablespoon olive oil
1 clove garlic, crushed
1 teaspoon finely grated lemon rind
½ teaspoon sweet paprika
2 medium radicchio (400g), trimmed, quartered
250g red grape tomatoes, halved
1 medium yellow capsicum (200g),
    chopped coarsely
1 small red onion (100g), sliced thinly
paprika mayonnaise
½ cup (150g) mayonnaise
1 tablespoon lemon juice
1 teaspoon sweet paprika

1 Combine veal, oil, garlic, rind and paprika in medium bowl; refrigerate 3 hours or overnight.
2 Make paprika mayonnaise.
3 Cook veal on heated oiled grill plate (or grill or barbecue) until cooked as desired. Cover veal; stand 5 minutes then slice thinly.
4 Meanwhile, cook radicchio on heated oiled grill plate until heated through.
5 Combine veal and remaining ingredients in medium bowl.
6 Divide radicchio among serving plates; top with veal mixture, drizzle with mayonnaise.

paprika mayonnaise Combine ingredients in small bowl.

prep and cook time 20 minutes (+ refrigeration)
serves 4

nutritional count per serving 19.4g total fat
(2.6g saturated fat); 1584kJ (379 cal);
12.7g carbohydrate; 36.5g protein; 4.1g fibre

mains lamb

sumac lamb with roasted eggplant and truss tomato salad

1 large eggplant (500g)
cooking-oil spray
1 medium red onion (170g), sliced thickly
2 tablespoons red wine vinegar
1 tablespoon brown sugar
4 cloves garlic
50g butter, chopped
¼ cup (60ml) olive oil
1 tablespoon finely chopped fresh flat-leaf parsley
500g baby truss tomatoes
400g lamb backstraps
3 teaspoons sumac
80g baby rocket leaves
⅓ cup (55g) sultanas

1 Preheat oven to 220°C/200°C fan-forced.
2 Cut eggplant into four 1cm slices; coat with cooking-oil spray. Cook on heated grill plate (or grill or barbecue) until tender.
3 Combine onion, vinegar, sugar, garlic, butter and 2 tablespoons of the oil in large shallow baking dish. Roast, in oven, stirring once, 10 minutes. Remove from oven, stir in parsley; cool 5 minutes.
4 Meanwhile, place tomatoes on oven tray; drizzle with remaining oil. Roast 10 minutes.
5 Rub lamb with sumac; cook on heated oiled grill plate (or grill or barbecue) until cooked as desired. Cover lamb; stand 5 minutes then slice thickly.
6 Combine rocket, sultanas and onion mixture in large bowl. Divide eggplant among serving plates; top with rocket mixture, lamb and tomatoes.
prep and cook time 45 minutes **serves** 4
nutritional count per serving *30.3g total fat (10.4g saturated fat); 1969kJ (471 cal); 22.6g carbohydrate; 24.3g protein; 6.9g fibre*

peppered lamb with watercress, pea and mint salad

2 tablespoons mixed peppercorns
1 tablespoon olive oil
600g lamb fillets
1 cup (160g) fresh or frozen peas
250g yellow teardrop tomatoes, halved
100g watercress, trimmed
200g fetta cheese, cut into thin strips
¼ cup coarsely chopped fresh mint
white wine vinaigrette
¼ cup (60ml) white wine vinegar
1 tablespoon olive oil
1 clove garlic, crushed

1 Using mortar and pestle, crush peppercorns until ground coarsely. Combine ground peppercorns, oil and lamb in medium bowl. Cook lamb in heated oiled large frying pan until cooked as desired. Cover lamb; stand 5 minutes then slice thinly.
2 Meanwhile, make white wine vinaigrette.
3 Boil, steam or microwave peas until tender; drain. Rinse under cold water; drain.
4 Combine lamb, peas, vinaigrette and remaining ingredients in large bowl.
white wine vinaigrette Combine ingredients in screw-top jar; shake well.

prep and cook time 30 minutes **serves** *4*
nutritional count per serving 31.1g total fat (12g saturated fat); 2006kJ (480 cal); 5.1g carbohydrate; 43.2g protein; 5g fibre

beetroot salad with honey balsamic lamb

800g lamb fillets
1 tablespoon honey
1 tablespoon balsamic vinegar
1 clove garlic, crushed
500g baby beetroot
2 teaspoons olive oil
1 lebanese cucumber (130g), seeded, sliced thinly
200g ricotta cheese, crumbled
honey balsamic dressing
¼ cup (60ml) olive oil
2 tablespoons balsamic vinegar
1 tablespoon honey
1 teaspoon dijon mustard

1 Combine lamb, honey, vinegar and garlic in medium bowl; cover, refrigerate 3 hours or overnight.
2 Preheat oven to 220°C/200°C fan-forced.
3 Remove unblemished leaves from the beetroot, reserve for later use. Peel and quarter beetroot. Place on oven tray; drizzle with oil. Roast, uncovered, about 30 minutes or until tender.
4 Meanwhile, cook lamb in heated oiled large frying pan until cooked as desired. Cover lamb; stand 5 minutes then slice thinly.
5 Make honey balsamic dressing.
6 Combine lamb, beetroot, beetroot leaves, cucumber and dressing in large bowl; sprinkle with cheese.
honey balsamic dressing Combine ingredients in small bowl.

prep and cook time 40 minutes (+ refrigeration) *serves 4*
nutritional count per serving 28.9g total fat (9.1g saturated fat); 2228kJ (533 cal); 19.2g carbohydrate; 47.9g protein; 2.8g fibre

barbecued lamb, shallot and mesclun salad

150g sugar snap peas, trimmed
600g lamb backstrap
8 large shallots (200g), peeled, quartered
60g mesclun
mint dressing
1 cup firmly packed fresh mint leaves
2 cloves garlic, quartered
¼ cup (60ml) olive oil
2 tablespoons white wine vinegar
2 teaspoons caster sugar

1 Boil, steam or microwave peas until tender; drain.
2 Meanwhile, cook lamb and shallot on heated oiled grill plate
(or grill or barbecue) until lamb is cooked as desired and onions
are tender. Cover lamb; stand 5 minutes then slice thinly.
3 Make mint dressing.
4 Combine peas, lamb, shallot, dressing and mesclun in large bowl.
mint dressing Blend or process mint and garlic until smooth. With
motor operating, gradually add oil in a thin, steady stream; blend
until smooth. Stir in vinegar and sugar.
prep and cook time *25 minutes* **serves** *4*
nutritional count per serving *19.4g total fat (4.4g saturated fat);*
1404kJ (336 cal); 6.2g carbohydrate; 33.2g protein; 2.7g fibre

mains pork

pork belly and nashi salad

1kg boneless pork belly, rind on
2 teaspoons sea salt flakes
750g choy sum, trimmed, sliced thinly
2 medium nashi (400g), cut into matchsticks
2 green onions, sliced thinly
1 fresh long red chilli, cut into matchsticks
plum and five-spice dressing
¼ cup (60ml) vegetable oil
2 tablespoons rice vinegar
1 tablespoon plum sauce
½ teaspoon five-spice powder

1 Score pork rind at 1cm intervals; rub salt all over pork rind. Place pork, rind-side up, on wire rack over large baking dish. Cover loosely; refrigerate overnight.
2 Preheat oven to 220°C/200°C fan-forced.
3 Roast pork, uncovered, 45 minutes. Reduce oven temperature to 180°C/160°C fan-forced. Roast pork, uncovered, a further 30 minutes or until rind is crisp and pork is cooked as desired. Stand pork, uncovered, 5 minutes then slice thinly.
4 Meanwhile, make plum and five-spice dressing.
5 Combine choy sum, nashi, onion and chilli in large bowl with half the dressing.
6 Divide salad among serving plates; top with pork, drizzle with remaining dressing.
plum and five-spice dressing Combine ingredients in screw-top jar; shake well.
prep and cook time *1 hour 30 minutes (+ refrigeration)* ***serves*** *6*
nutritional count per serving *46.7g total fat (13.8g saturated fat); 2462kJ (589 cal); 9.8g carbohydrate; 31.8g protein; 2.9g fibre*

Rubbing salt on the pork and leaving it overnight draws moisture out of the rind, drying it out – this helps to make perfect crackling. Ask your butcher to score the rind as they have the best tools for the job.
Five-spice powder is a fragrant spice mix often used in Asian cooking. It varies from country to country, but it usually includes ground cinnamon, cloves, star anise, sichuan pepper and fennel seeds. You need to buy 3 bunches of choy sum.

chorizo, roasted capsicum and artichoke salad

2 large red capsicums (700g)
2 chorizo sausages (340g), sliced thinly
280g jar artichoke hearts in brine, drained, halved
200g red grape tomatoes, halved
80g curly endive leaves
½ cup firmly packed fresh flat-leaf parsley leaves
herb and garlic dressing
2 tablespoons olive oil
2 tablespoons white wine vinegar
1 tablespoon lemon juice
1 tablespoon finely chopped fresh basil
1 tablespoon finely chopped fresh oregano
2 cloves garlic, chopped finely

1 Quarter capsicums; discard seeds and membranes. Roast capsicum under hot grill, skin-side up, until skin blisters and blackens. Cover capsicum pieces with plastic or paper for 5 minutes; peel away skin then cut pieces in half diagonally.
2 Meanwhile, cook chorizo in large frying pan, stirring occasionally, until browned. Drain on absorbent paper.
3 Make herb and garlic dressing.
4 Combine capsicum, chorizo, dressing and remaining ingredients in large bowl.
herb and garlic dressing Combine ingredients in small bowl.

prep and cook time 25 minutes **serves** *4*
nutritional count per serving *36g total fat (10.8g saturated fat); 1885kJ (451 cal); 16.4g carbohydrate; 20.5g protein; 3.9g fibre*

pork and caramelised apple salad

600g pork fillet
2 tablespoons brown sugar
2 teaspoons wholegrain mustard
2 teaspoons finely grated orange rind
1 tablespoon olive oil
10g butter
1 medium green-skinned apple (150g), unpeeled, halved, cut into 5mm-thick slices
60g baby spinach leaves
spiced orange dressing
¼ cup (60ml) olive oil
2 tablespoons orange juice
1 tablespoon cider vinegar
1 teaspoon mixed spice

1 Combine pork, sugar, mustard and rind in medium bowl.
2 Heat oil in medium frying pan; cook pork until cooked as desired. Cover pork; stand 5 minutes then slice thinly.
3 Melt butter in same frying pan; cook apple until caramelised.
4 Meanwhile, make spiced orange dressing.
5 Combine apple mixture, dressing and spinach in medium bowl. Arrange pork among serving plates; top with apple salad. Drizzle with any remaining dressing from bowl.
spiced orange dressing Combine ingredients in screw-top jar; shake well.

prep and cook time 30 minutes **serves** *4*
nutritional count per serving *23.8g total fat (5.1g saturated fat); 1639kJ (392 cal); 10.6g carbohydrate; 33.5g protein; 1.1g fibre*

mains
pulses & grains

chickpea, pumpkin and fetta salad

800g butternut pumpkin, cut into 1cm pieces
1 tablespoon olive oil
2 cloves garlic, sliced thinly
2 x 400g cans chickpeas, rinsed, drained
200g fetta cheese, crumbled
1 cup firmly packed fresh coriander leaves
⅓ cup (65g) pepitas
roasted chilli dressing
4 fresh long red chillies, halved lengthways
2 tablespoons rice vinegar
2 tablespoons lime juice
1 tablespoon olive oil

1 Preheat oven to 200°C/180°C fan-forced.
2 Combine pumpkin, oil and garlic in large shallow baking dish. Roast, uncovered, turning occasionally, about 30 minutes or until pumpkin is tender.
3 Meanwhile, make roasted chilli dressing.
4 Combine pumpkin, dressing and remaining ingredients in large bowl.
roasted chilli dressing Cook chilli, skin-side up, under hot grill until skin blackens. Cover chilli pieces for 5 minutes; peel then chop finely. Combine chilli and remaining ingredients in screw-top jar; shake well.
prep and cook time 40 minutes serves 4
nutritional count per serving 31.7g total fat (11.2g saturated fat); 2195kJ (525 cal); 32.3g carbohydrate; 25.2g protein; 9.5g fibre

Greek-style yogurt is
especially thick and
creamy – perfect to use
in this dressing with the
lemon juice and rind.

tuna, bean and haloumi salad

500g spinach, trimmed
250g haloumi cheese, cut lengthways
   into 1cm slices
2 x 420g cans four-bean mix, rinsed, drained
425g can tuna in oil, drained, flaked
250g yellow grape tomatoes, halved
creamy lemon dressing
½ cup (140g) greek-style yogurt
½ teaspoon finely grated lemon rind
1 teaspoon dijon mustard
¼ cup (60ml) lemon juice

1 Boil, steam or microwave spinach until wilted; drain, chop coarsely.
2 Meanwhile, make creamy lemon dressing.
3 Cook cheese in heated oiled large frying pan until browned lightly.
4 Combine spinach, beans, tuna and tomato in large bowl. Divide salad among serving bowls; top with cheese, drizzle with dressing. Serve with lemon wedges, if you like.
creamy lemon dressing Combine ingredients in small bowl.
prep and cook time *30 minutes* ***serves*** *4*
nutritional count per serving *25.8g total fat (10.5g saturated fat); 2278kJ (545 cal); 25.6g carbohydrate; 47.1g protein; 11.4g fibre*

brown lentil, zucchini and chorizo salad

2 chorizo sausages (340g), sliced thinly
1 large zucchini (150g), sliced thinly lengthways
2 x 400g cans brown lentils, rinsed, drained
250g red grape tomatoes, halved
1 cup loosely packed fresh flat-leaf parsley leaves
cajun dressing
¼ cup (60ml) olive oil
1 tablespoon red wine vinegar
2 tablespoons cajun spice mix

1 Cook chorizo and zucchini on heated oiled grill plate (or grill or barbecue) until chorizo is cooked and zucchini is tender.
2 Meanwhile, make cajun dressing.
3 Combine chorizo, zucchini, dressing and remaining ingredients in large bowl.
cajun dressing Combine ingredients in screw-top jar; shake well.
prep and cook time *30 minutes* ***serves*** *4*
nutritional count per serving *39.8g total fat (11.2g saturated fat); 2161kJ (517 cal); 13.9g carbohydrate; 24.1g protein; 6.2g fibre*

red lentil patty salad

1 cup (200g) red lentils
¼ cup (40g) burghul
½ cup (125ml) boiling water
1 small brown onion (80g), chopped coarsely
2 cloves garlic, quartered
⅔ cup (100g) plain flour
1 egg
1 cup (100g) packaged breadcrumbs
2 tablespoons olive oil
1 cup loosely packed fresh flat-leaf parsley leaves
3 medium tomatoes (450g) cut into wedges
1 lebanese cucumber (130g), chopped coarsely
1 medium avocado (250g), chopped coarsely
1 small green capsicum (150g), sliced thinly
lemon yogurt dressing
1 cup (280g) yogurt
2 teaspoons finely grated lemon rind
2 tablespoons lemon juice

1 Cook lentils in medium saucepan of boiling water until tender; drain, cool.
2 Meanwhile, place burghul in small heatproof bowl; cover with the water. Stand 10 minutes.
3 Blend or process lentils, onion and garlic until smooth; transfer to medium bowl. Stir in burghul, flour, egg and breadcrumbs. Refrigerate 1 hour or until firm.
4 Meanwhile, make lemon yogurt dressing.
5 Shape lentil mixture into 20 patties. Heat oil in large frying pan; cook patties until browned. Drain on absorbent paper.
6 Combine patties with remaining ingredients in large bowl; drizzle with dressing.
lemon yogurt dressing Combine ingredients in small bowl.

prep and cook time 20 minutes
(+ cooling and refrigeration) **serves** 4
nutritional count per serving 25.3g total fat (5.8g saturated fat); 2675kJ (640 cal); 68g carbohydrate; 27.6g protein; 14.4g fibre

bean salad with creamy basil dressing

400g can butter beans, rinsed, drained
400g can borlotti beans, rinsed, drained
250g cherry tomatoes, quartered
12 cherry bocconcini cheese (180g), halved
60g baby rocket leaves
½ cup (80g) roasted pine nuts
creamy basil dressing
2 tablespoons olive oil
2 tablespoons white wine vinegar
2 teaspoons white balsamic vinegar
2 tablespoons coarsely chopped fresh basil leaves
¼ cup (60ml) cream

1 Make creamy basil dressing.
2 Combine salad ingredients with dressing in large bowl.
creamy basil dressing Combine oil, vinegars and basil in small bowl. Add cream; whisk until combined.
prep time *15 minutes* ***serves*** *4*
nutritional count per serving *37.1g total fat (11g saturated fat); 1944kJ (465 cal); 13g carbohydrate; 17.1g protein; 7.7g fibre*

crispy polenta, capsicum and walnut salad

1 litre (4 cups) water
1 cup (170g) polenta
½ cup (40g) coarsely grated parmesan cheese
½ cup (60g) coarsely grated cheddar cheese
1 tablespoon olive oil
80g baby spinach leaves
1 large red capsicum (350g), sliced thinly
1 small red onion (100g), sliced thinly
walnut dressing
¼ cup (60ml) walnut oil
2 tablespoons white wine vinegar
1 clove garlic, crushed
⅓ cup (35g) coarsely chopped roasted walnuts
¼ cup coarsely chopped fresh flat-leaf parsley

1 Oil 19cm x 29cm slice pan.
2 Bring the water to the boil in medium saucepan. Gradually stir in polenta; reduce heat. Simmer, stirring, about 10 minutes or until polenta thickens. Stir in cheeses; spread polenta into pan. Refrigerate 1 hour or until firm.
3 Meanwhile make walnut dressing.
4 Turn polenta onto board; cut into quarters then cut into 1cm cubes. Heat oil in large frying pan; cook polenta until browned lightly.
5 Combine polenta, dressing and remaining ingredients in large bowl.
walnut dressing Combine ingredients in screw-top jar; shake well.
prep and cook time *25 minutes (+ refrigeration)* ***serves*** *4*
nutritional count per serving *25g total fat (7.1g saturated fat); 1831kJ (438 cal); 35g carbohydrate; 16.4g protein; 4.6g fibre*

mains
cheese & eggs

bocconcini salad with semi-dried tomato pesto

270g jar semi-dried tomatoes in oil
¼ cup (20g) coarsely grated parmesan cheese
1 tablespoon roasted pine nuts
1 fresh long red chilli, chopped coarsely
2 tablespoons lemon juice
⅓ cup (80ml) cream
630g cherry bocconcini cheese, drained
1 cup (150g) plain flour
2 eggs, beaten lightly
1 cup (100g) packaged breadcrumbs
vegetable oil, for deep-frying
4 white witlof (500g), trimmed
¼ cup mizuna

1 Drain tomatoes over small bowl; reserve ½ cup of the oil. Roughly chop half the tomatoes; slice remaining tomatoes into thin strips.
2 Blend chopped tomatoes, parmesan, nuts, chilli and juice until smooth. With motor operating, gradually add reserved oil in a thin, steady stream; blend until smooth. Transfer pesto to small jug; stir in cream.
3 Coat bocconcini in flour; shake off excess. Dip in egg, then coat in breadcrumbs.
4 Heat oil in medium deep saucepan; deep-fry bocconcini, in batches, until browned lightly. Drain on absorbent paper.
5 Divide witlof among serving plates; top with bocconcini then sprinkle with sliced tomato and mizuna. Drizzle over pesto to serve.
prep and cook time *45 minutes* **serves** *4*
nutritional count per serving *52.5g total fat (25.1g saturated fat); 3867kJ (925 cal); 60.7g carbohydrate; 47g protein; 11.5g fibre*

You need to buy three tubs of cherry bocconcini cheese for this recipe.

poached egg, asparagus and walnut salad

500g asparagus, trimmed, halved
½ cup (55g) coarsely chopped roasted walnuts
½ cup (40g) coarsely grated parmesan cheese
250g yellow teardrop tomatoes, halved
8 eggs
1 small french bread stick (150g), sliced thinly
lime, garlic and dill dressing
¼ cup (60ml) olive oil
2 teaspoons finely grated lime rind
1 tablespoon lime juice
1 clove garlic, crushed
2 teaspoons finely chopped fresh dill

1 Make lime, garlic and dill dressing.
2 Boil, steam or microwave asparagus until tender; drain. Combine asparagus, nuts, cheese, tomato and dressing in medium bowl. Divide asparagus mixture among serving plates.
3 Poach eggs until barely set. Toast bread.
4 Top salad with eggs, serve with toast.
lime, garlic and dill dressing Combine ingredients in screw-top jar; shake well.
prep and cook time *20 minutes* ***serves*** *4*
nutritional count per serving *38.5g total fat (8g saturated fat); 2282kJ (546 cal); 23.4g carbohydrate; 25.1g protein; 4.8g fibre*

roasted root vegetable salad with lemon and fetta

500g baby new potatoes, unpeeled, halved
500g butternut pumpkin, chopped coarsely
4 small beetroot (400g), peeled
1 medium parsnip (250g), quartered
400g baby carrots, trimmed
1 medium lemon (140g), sliced thinly
2 tablespoons olive oil
30g butter, chopped
2 tablespoons fresh oregano leaves
2 tablespoons lemon juice
1 tablespoon wholegrain mustard
100g baby rocket leaves
100g fetta cheese, crumbled

1 Preheat oven to 200°C/180°C fan-forced.
2 Combine potato, pumpkin, beetroot, parsnip, carrots, lemon, oil, butter and half the oregano in large shallow baking dish. Roast, uncovered, turning occasionally, about 40 minutes or until vegetables are tender.
3 Meanwhile, combine juice and mustard in screw-top jar; shake well.
4 Combine vegetables with mustard mixture and rocket in large bowl; sprinkle over cheese and remaining oregano leaves.
prep and cook time *50 minutes* ***serves*** *4*
nutritional count per serving *22.2g total fat (9.5g saturated fat); 1881kJ (450 cal); 42.6g carbohydrate; 14g protein; 12.2g fibre*

Lemon myrtle is a small tree that grows in sub-tropical and tropical rainforest areas of Queensland. Ground lemon myrtle is a ground mixture of the dried leaf and flower; it has a strong lemon flavour. If you can't find it, use 1 teaspoon finely grated lemon rind instead.

pumpkin, ricotta, beetroot and pecan salad

4 baby beetroot (100g)
800g pumpkin, unpeeled, cut into 8 wedges
2 tablespoons olive oil
40g mesclun
1 cup (120g) coarsely chopped roasted pecans
200g ricotta cheese, crumbled
lemon myrtle dressing
1 tablespoon cider vinegar
1 tablespoon lemon juice
1 teaspoon ground lemon myrtle
2 tablespoons olive oil

1 Preheat oven to 200°C/180°C fan-forced.
2 Remove unblemished leaves from beetroot, reserve. Peel and halve beetroot.
3 Combine beetroot, pumpkin and oil in large shallow baking dish. Roast, uncovered, turning occasionally, about 40 minutes or until vegetables are tender.
4 Meanwhile, make lemon myrtle dressing.
5 Combine vegetables, beetroot leaves, mesclun, nuts and cheese in large bowl; drizzle with dressing.
lemon myrtle dressing Combine ingredients in screw-top jar; shake well.
prep and cook time *45 minutes* ***serves*** *4*
nutritional count per serving *37.5g total fat (6.8g saturated fat); 1885kJ (451 cal); 14.7g carbohydrate; 12.2g protein; 3.4g fibre*

Ground lemon myrtle is available from specialist spice shops and some gourmet food stores.

egg and bacon salad

1 medium kumara (400g), cut into 2cm pieces
cooking-oil spray
4 rindless bacon rashers (260g)
6 hard-boiled eggs, quartered
1 stalk celery (150g), trimmed, sliced thinly
80g mesclun
honey mustard dressing
½ cup (140g) mayonnaise
¼ cup (60ml) cider vinegar
1 tablespoon honey
2 teaspoons wholegrain mustard

1 Preheat oven to 220°C/200°C fan-forced.
2 Place kumara on oven tray; spray with cooking oil. Roast, uncovered, about 20 minutes or until tender.
3 Meanwhile, cook bacon in heated large frying pan; drain on absorbent paper. Chop coarsely.
4 Make honey mustard dressing.
5 Combine kumara, bacon, dressing and remaining ingredients in large bowl.
honey mustard dressing Combine ingredients in small bowl.
prep and cook time *25 minutes* ***serves*** *4*
nutritional count per serving *29.2g total fat (6.9g saturated fat); 1965kJ (470 cal); 25.9g carbohydrate; 25g protein; 2.6g fibre*

grilled goats cheese salad

1 small french bread stick (150g), sliced thinly
2 tablespoons olive oil
½ cup (50g) roasted walnuts, coarsely chopped
⅓ cup coarsely chopped fresh flat-leaf parsley
1 clove garlic, chopped finely
2 tablespoons walnut oil
1 tablespoon white wine vinegar
300g log goats cheese (with rind), cut into 4 slices
80g mesclun

1 Brush bread with olive oil; cook on heated oiled grill plate (or grill or barbecue) until browned both sides.
2 Meanwhile, combine nuts, parsley, garlic, walnut oil and vinegar in small bowl.
3 Preheat grill. Place cheese slices on oven tray; cook, under grill, until browned lightly.
4 Divide mesclun among serving plates; top with cheese and walnut mixture, serve with bread.
prep and cook time *20 minutes* ***serves*** *4*
nutritional count per serving *34.4g total fat (10.2g saturated fat); 1952kJ (467 cal); 21.8g carbohydrate; 16.6g protein; 3.5g fibre*

dressings

thousand island dressing

½ cup (150g) mayonnaise
1½ tablespoons tomato sauce
½ small white onion (40g), grated finely
8 pimiento-stuffed green olives, chopped finely
½ small red capsicum (75g), chopped finely

1 Combine ingredients in small bowl.
prep time 10 minutes **makes** *1 cup*
nutritional count per tablespoon *4.3g total fat*
(0.5g saturated fat); 226kJ (54 cal);
3.6g carbohydrate; 0.3g protein; 0.4g fibre

sweet chilli dressing

2 tablespoons fish sauce
2 tablespoons sweet chilli sauce
⅓ cup (80ml) lime juice
1 fresh long red chilli, chopped finely
1 tablespoon grated palm sugar

1 Combine ingredients in screw-top jar; shake well.
prep time 5 minutes **makes** *⅔ cup*
nutritional count per tablespoon *0.1g total fat*
(0g saturated fat); 71kJ (17 cal);
3g carbohydrate; 0.6g protein; 0.3g fibre

creamy oregano and caper dressing

2 hard-boiled eggs, quartered
1 tablespoon rinsed, drained capers
2 tablespoons white wine vinegar
2 tablespoons coarsely chopped fresh oregano
1 clove garlic, quartered
⅓ cup (80ml) olive oil

1 Blend or process egg, capers, vinegar, oregano and garlic until smooth. With motor operating, add oil in a thin, steady stream; blend until dressing thickens.
prep time *10 minutes* ***makes*** *1 cup*
nutritional count per tablespoon *7g total fat (1.1g saturated fat); 280kJ (67 cal); 0.2g carbohydrate; 1.1g protein; 0.1g fibre*

rosemary balsamic dressing

2 tablespoons olive oil
1 tablespoon balsamic vinegar
1 tablespoon lemon juice
1 tablespoon coarsely chopped fresh rosemary

1 Combine ingredients in screw-top jar; shake well.
prep time *10 minutes* ***makes*** *⅓ cup*
nutritional count per tablespoon *9.1g total fat (1.3g saturated fat); 339kJ (81 cal); 0.1g carbohydrate; 0g protein; 0g fibre*

mayonnaise

2 egg yolks
½ teaspoon salt
1 teaspoon dijon mustard
⅔ cup (160ml) extra light olive oil
⅓ cup (80ml) olive oil
1 tablespoon white wine vinegar
1 tablespoon lemon juice

1 Combine egg yolks, salt and mustard in medium bowl. Gradually add oils in a thin, steady stream, whisking constantly until mixture thickens. Stir in vinegar and juice.
prep time *15 minutes* **makes** *1 cup*
nutritional count per tablespoon *19.2g total fat (2.9g saturated fat); 719kJ (172 cal); 0g carbohydrate; 0.5g protein; 0g fibre*

ranch dressing

½ cup (150g) mayonnaise
¼ cup (60ml) buttermilk
1 tablespoon white wine vinegar
1 small brown onion (80g), chopped finely
1 clove garlic, crushed
1 tablespoon finely chopped fresh chives
1 tablespoon finely chopped fresh flat-leaf parsley
¼ teaspoon sweet paprika

1 Whisk ingredients in small jug until combined.
prep time *10 minutes* **makes** *1 cup*
nutritional count per tablespoon *4.2g total fat (0.5g saturated fat); 217kJ (52 cal); 3.2g carbohydrate; 0.5g protein; 0.2g fibre*

lemon and macadamia dressing

½ cup (125ml) macadamia oil
⅓ cup (45g) finely chopped roasted
   unsalted macadamias
2 teaspoons finely grated lemon rind
2 tablespoons lemon juice
1 teaspoon caster sugar

1 Whisk ingredients in small jug until combined.
prep time *10 minutes* ***makes*** *1 cup*
nutritional count per tablespoon *12.4g total fat*
(1.8g saturated fat); 477kJ (114 cal);
0.6g carbohydrate; 0.3g protein; 0.2g fibre

citrus and poppy seed dressing

2 teaspoons finely grated orange rind
¼ cup (60ml) orange juice
2 tablespoons cider vinegar
1 tablespoon poppy seeds
⅓ cup (80g) sour cream
2 teaspoons honey mustard
¼ cup (60ml) water

1 Whisk rind, juice, vinegar, seeds, sour cream
and mustard in small bowl. Add the water; whisk
until combined.
prep time *10 minutes* ***makes*** *1 cup*
nutritional count per tablespoon *3.1g total fat*
(1.8g saturated fat); 134kJ (32 cal);
0.7g carbohydrate; 0.4g protein; 0.2g fibre

glossary

BALMAIN BUG a type of crayfish; also known as shovelnose, southern bay or slipper lobster. Substitute with moreton bay bugs, king prawns or scampi.

BEANS

black also known as turtle beans or black kidney beans; jet black with a tiny white eye. An earthy-flavoured dried bean completely different from the better-known chinese black beans (which are fermented soya beans). Can be found in some greengrocers and delicatessens.

borlotti also known as roman beans or pink beans; can be eaten fresh or dried. They are interchangeable with pinto beans because of the similarity in appearance – both are pale pink or beige with dark red streaks.

broad also known as fava, windsor and horse beans; available canned, frozen, dried and fresh. Fresh should be peeled twice (discarding both the outer long green pod and the beige-green tough inner shell); the frozen beans have had their pods removed, but the beige shell still needs removal.

butter also known as lima beans. Large, flat, kidney-shaped bean; off-white in colour with a mealy texture and mild taste.

cannellini a small white bean similar in appearance and flavour to haricot, navy and great northern beans.

kidney medium-sized red bean, slightly floury in texture yet sweet in flavour. Sold dried or canned.

lima also known as butter beans; large, flat, kidney-shaped bean, off-white in colour, with a mealy texture and mild taste.

snake long (about 40cm), thin, round, fresh green beans. Asian in origin, with a taste similar to green or french beans. Also known as yard-long beans because of their (pre-metric) length.

BEETROOT also known as red beets or beets; firm, round, root vegetable. Can be eaten raw, boiled or roasted.

BETEL LEAVES the leaf of the betel plant; commonly used in Asian cooking. Can be purchased from Asian grocers and some supermarkets and greengrocers. Most often used as a wrapper for spiced minced meat and other snack foods.

BLACK CUMIN SEEDS also known as jeera kala; often confused with kalonji (black onion or nigella seeds). Used extensively in Indian and Moroccan cooking to impart a distinctive "curry" flavour.

BREADCRUMBS

fresh white bread processed into crumbs.
packaged fine-textured, crunchy, purchased white breadcrumbs.

BURGHUL also known as bulghur or bulgar wheat; hulled steamed wheat kernels that, once dried, are crushed into various-sized grains. Used in Middle Eastern dishes such as felafel, kibbeh and tabbouleh. Burghul is not the same as cracked wheat. Found in most supermarkets and health-food stores.

CELERIAC tuberous root with knobbly brown skin, white flesh and a celery-like flavour. Keep peeled celeriac in acidulated water (water to which lemon juice has been added) to prevent cut surfaces from discolouring.

CHEESE

bocconcini walnut-sized baby mozzarella; a delicate, semi-soft, white cheese traditionally made from buffalo milk. Sold fresh, it spoils rapidly so will only keep, refrigerated in brine, for 2 days at the most.
fetta a crumbly textured goat-or sheep-milk cheese having a sharp, salty taste. Ripened and stored in salted whey.
haloumi has a semi-firm, spongy texture and very salty, yet sweet, flavour. Ripened and stored in salted whey; it's best grilled or fried, and holds its shape well when heated. Should be eaten while warm as it becomes tough and rubbery on cooling.
parmesan also known as parmigiano; a hard, grainy cows-milk cheese. The curd is salted in brine for a month before being aged for up to 2 years, preferably in humid conditions.
ricotta a soft, sweet, moist, white cows-milk cheese with a low fat content and a slightly grainy texture. The name roughly translates as "cooked again" and refers to ricotta's manufacture from a whey that is itself a by-product of other cheese making.

CHICKEN, SMOKED ready-to-eat; available, as a whole small bird or breast fillet, cryovac-packed in supermarkets.

CHINESE BARBECUED DUCK traditionally cooked in special ovens in China; dipped into and brushed during roasting with a sticky sweet coating made from soy sauce, sherry, ginger, five-spice, star anise and hoisin sauce. Available from Asian food shops as well as dedicated Chinese barbecued meat shops.

CHICKPEAS also called garbanzos, hummus or channa; an irregularly round, sandy-coloured legume. Retains a firm texture even after cooking; has a floury mouth-feel and robust nutty flavour. Available canned or dried (the latter need several hours reconstituting in cold water before being used).

CHOY SUM also known as pakaukeo or flowering cabbage, a member of the buk choy family; easy to identify with its long stems, light green leaves and yellow flowers. Stems and leaves are both edible.

CIABATTA in Italian, the word means slipper, the traditional shape of this popular crisp-crusted, open-textured white sourdough bread.

COCONUT CREAM obtained commercially from the first pressing of the coconut flesh alone, without the addition of water; the second pressing (less rich) is sold as coconut milk. Available in cans and cartons at most supermarkets.

COS LETTUCE also known as romaine lettuce; the traditional caesar salad lettuce. Long, with leaves ranging from dark green on the outside to almost white near the core; the leaves have a stiff centre rib that gives a slight cupping effect to the leaf on either side.

CRÈME FRAÎCHE a mature, naturally fermented cream having a velvety texture and slightly tangy, nutty flavour. Crème fraîche, a French variation of sour cream, can boil without curdling and can be used in both sweet and savoury dishes.

DRIED CRANBERRIES have the same slightly sour, succulent flavour as fresh cranberries; dried sweetened cranberries have the addition of a sweetener. They are available from supermarkets.

EGGPLANT purple-skinned vegetable also known as aubergine.
baby also known as finger or japanese eggplant; very small and slender so can be used without disgorging (salting to remove the bitter juices).

EGGS some recipes in this book may call for raw or barely cooked eggs; exercise caution if there is a salmonella problem in your area.

ENDIVE a curly salad green with irregular-shaped leaves.

FENNEL a roundish, bulbous vegetable, about 8-12cm in diameter, with a mild licorice smell and taste. Has a large white to very pale green, firm, crisp bulb. The bulb has a slightly sweet, anise flavour, but the leaves (fronds) have a much stronger taste. Also the name given to dried seeds having a licorice flavour.

GRISSINI thin Italian breadsticks; a common feature on antipasti plates.

HORSERADISH mainly grown for its long, pungent white root. Occasionally found fresh in specialty greengrocers and some Asian food shops, but most commonly purchased in bottles at the supermarket in two forms: prepared horseradish and horseradish cream. These cannot be substituted one for the other in cooking but both can be used as table condiments.
cream a commercially prepared creamy paste consisting of grated horseradish, vinegar, oil and sugar.
prepared the preserved grated root.

KAFFIR LIME LEAF also known as bai magrood; looks like two glossy dark green leaves joined end to end, forming a rounded hourglass shape. Used fresh or dried like bay leaves or curry leaves. Sold fresh, dried or frozen, the dried leaves are less potent so double the number if using them as a substitute for fresh; a strip of fresh lime peel may be substituted for each kaffir lime leaf.

KECAP MANIS see sauces.

KUMARA the Polynesian name of an orange-fleshed sweet potato often confused with yam.

LAMB'S LETTUCE also known as corn salad or mâche; has a mild, almost nutty flavour and dark green leaves.

LAVASH flat, unleavened bread of Mediterranean origin; good used as a wrapper or torn and used for dips.

LEMON MYRTLE a flowering plant native to Australia with strong, lemon-scented leaves.

LYCHEES a small fruit from China with a hard shell and sweet, juicy flesh. The white flesh has a gelatinous texture and musky, perfumed taste. Discard the rough skin and seed before using. Also available canned in a sugar syrup.

MANGO, GREEN sour and crunchy, green mangoes are just immature fruit. They will keep, wrapped in plastic, in the fridge for up to two weeks. Available from Asian food stores, greengrocers and some supermarkets.

MESCLUN (mess-kluhn); also known as mixed greens or spring salad mix. A commercial mix of assorted young lettuce and other green leaves, including baby spinach leaves, mizuna and curly endive.

MIRIN a Japanese champagne-coloured cooking wine made of glutinous rice and alcohol. It is used expressly for cooking and should not be confused with sake.

MIZUNA Japanese in origin; wispy, feathered, green salad leaves having a delicate mustard flavour.

MUSHROOM, FLAT large and flat with a rich, earthy flavour, these mushrooms are ideal for filling and barbecuing. Are sometimes misnamed field mushrooms, which are wild mushrooms.

NASHI a member of the pear family but resembling an apple with its pale yellow-green, tennis-ball-sized appearance; more commonly known as the asian pear to much of the world. The nashi is different from other pears in that it is crisp, juicy and ready to eat as soon as it is picked and for several months thereafter, unlike its European cousins.

NOODLES
dried rice also known as rice stick noodles. Made from rice flour and water; available flat and wide or very thin (vermicelli). Must be soaked in boiling water to soften.

soba thin, pale-brown noodle originally from Japan; made from buckwheat and varying proportions of wheat flour. Available dried and fresh, and in flavoured varieties, such as green tea. Can be eaten in soups, stir-fries and, chilled, on their own.

NORI a type of dried seaweed used in Japanese cooking as a flavouring, garnish or for sushi. Sold in thin sheets, plain or toasted (yaki-nori).

OIL
macadamia pressed from ground macadamias; store in the refrigerator to prevent the oil from turning rancid.
olive made from ripened olives. Extra virgin and virgin are the best, while extra light or light refers to taste not fat levels.
peanut pressed from ground peanuts; the most commonly used oil in Asian cooking because of its high smoke point (capacity to handle high heat without burning).
sesame made from roasted, crushed, white sesame seeds; a flavouring rather than a cooking medium.
vegetable sourced from plants rather than animal fats.
walnut pressed from ground walnuts; commonly used in salad dressings. Store in the refrigerator to prevent the oil from turning rancid.

PALM SUGAR also known as nam tan pip, jaggery, jawa or gula melaka; made from the sap of the sugar palm tree. Light brown to black in colour and usually sold in rock-hard cakes; substitute with brown sugar, if unavailable.

PAPAYA, GREEN (pawpaw) these are just unripe papayas. They are available from Asian food stores; look for one that is hard and slightly shiny, proving it is freshly picked. Papaya will ripen rapidly if not used within a day or two.

PEPITAS also known as pumpkin seed kernels; the pale green kernels of dried pumpkin seeds. Available plain or salted.

PICKLED GINGER available packaged from Asian grocery stores; pickled, paper-thin shavings of ginger in a mixture of vinegar, sugar and natural colouring. It is used in cooking and as a condiment.

POMEGRANATE the fruit of a large bush native to the Middle-East region, although it is now grown in other regions around the world. A dark-red, leathery-skinned fruit, about the size of an orange, filled with hundreds of seeds, each wrapped in an edible lucent-crimson pulp having a tangy sweet-sour flavour.

POTATO
baby new also known as chats; not a separate variety but an early harvest with very thin skin, so there is no need to peel them before using.
desiree oval, smooth and pink-skinned with a waxy yellow flesh.
kipfler a small, finger-shaped potato with a nutty flavour.

PRESERVED LEMONS a North African specialty; lemons are preserved in salt and lemon juice or water. To use, remove and discard pulp; squeeze juice from rind, rinse rind well then slice. Sold in jars or in bulk by delicatessens; once opened, store preserved lemon in the refrigerator. Adds a rich, salty-sour flavour to dishes.

PROSCIUTTO a kind of unsmoked Italian ham; salted, air-cured and aged, it is usually eaten uncooked. There are many styles of prosciutto, one of the best being Parma ham, from Italy's Emilia Romagna region.

RADICCHIO Italian in origin; a member of the chicory family. The dark burgundy leaves have a strong, bitter flavour.

RAS EL HANOUT is a classic spice blend used in Moroccan cooking. The name means "top of the shop", or the very best spice blend that a spice merchant has to offer. Most versions contain over a dozen spices, including cardamom, mace, nutmeg, cinnamon, and ground chilli.

ROCKET also known as arugula, rugula and rucola; a peppery green leaf eaten raw in salads or used in cooking. Baby rocket leaves, also known as wild rocket, are smaller and less peppery.

SAUCES
fish also known as naam pla or nuoc naam. Made from pulverised salted fermented fish (most often anchovies); has a pungent smell and strong taste. Available in varying degrees of intensity, so use according to your taste.

kecap manis a dark, thick sweet soy sauce. The sweetness is derived from the addition of either molasses or palm sugar when brewed. Use as a condiment, dipping sauce, ingredient or marinade.
soy also known as sieu; made from fermented soya beans. Several variations are available in supermarkets and Asian food stores; we use japanese soy sauce unless indicated otherwise.
dark soy is deep brown, almost black in colour; it is rich, with a thicker consistency than other types. Pungent, although not particularly salty, it is good for marinating.
japanese soy is an all-purpose low-sodium sauce made with more wheat than its Chinese counterparts. Possibly the best table soy and the one to choose if you only want one variety.
light soy has a fairly thin consistency and, while paler than the others, is the saltiest tasting. It's used in dishes in which the natural colour of the ingredients is to be maintained. Not to be confused with salt-reduced or low-sodium soy sauces.

SUMAC purple-red, astringent spice ground from berries growing on shrubs that flourish wild around the Mediterranean; adds a tart, lemony flavour. Found in Middle-Eastern food stores.

TAMARIND CONCENTRATE (or paste) the commercial result of the distillation of tamarind juice into a condensed, compacted paste. Can be used straight from the container, with no soaking or straining required, or can be diluted with water according to taste. Found in Asian grocery stores and some supermarkets.

TATSOI also known as rosette, pak choy and chinese flat cabbage; a member of the same family as buk choy, it has the same mild flavour. The smaller, more delicate leaves are usually eaten in salads, while the larger leaves may be used in soups, curries and stir-fries.

THAI BASIL also known as horapa; different from sweet (common) basil in both look and taste, having smaller leaves and purplish stems. It has a sweet licorice/aniseed taste.

TOMATO
baby truss small vine-ripened tomatoes with the vine still attached.

cherry also known as tiny tim or tom thumb tomatoes; small and round.
egg also called plum or roma, these are smallish, oval-shaped tomatoes much used in Italian cooking or salads.
grape are about the size of a grape; they can be oblong, pear or grape-shaped and are often used whole in salads or eaten as a snack.
green simply under-ripe tomatoes.
teardrop slightly smaller than cherry tomatoes but pear-shaped; are either red or yellow in colour.

VIETNAMESE MINT not a mint at all, but a pungent and peppery narrow-leafed member of the buckwheat family.

VINEGAR
balsamic made from the juice of Trebbiano grapes; it is a deep rich-brown colour with a sweet/sour flavour. Quality can be determined up to a point by price; use the most expensive sparingly.
cider (apple cider) made from fermented apples.
malt (brown malt) made from fermented malt and beech shavings.
raspberry made from fresh raspberries steeped in a white wine vinegar.
red wine made from red wine.
rice wine made from fermented rice.
white balsamic made from grape must (the juice pressed from grapes before they ferment; new wine) and white wine vinegar. Has a fresh, sweet clean taste.
white wine made from white wine.

WASABI an Asian horseradish used to make the pungent, green-coloured condiment; sold powdered or as a paste.

WATERCRESS one of the cress family, a large group of peppery greens. Highly perishable, so must be used as soon as possible after purchase.

WOMBOK also known as chinese, peking or napa cabbage; elongated in shape with pale green, crinkly leaves, this is the most common cabbage in South-East Asia.

WONTON WRAPPERS made of flour, egg and water; are found in the freezer or refrigerated section of Asian food shops and many supermarkets. They come in different thicknesses, sizes and shapes (round or square).

conversion chart

MEASURES

One Australian metric measuring cup holds approximately 250ml; one Australian metric tablespoon holds 20ml; one Australian metric teaspoon holds 5ml.

The difference between one country's measuring cups and another's is within a two- or three-teaspoon variance, and will not affect your cooking results. North America, New Zealand and the United Kingdom use a 15ml tablespoon.

All cup and spoon measurements are level. The most accurate way of measuring dry ingredients is to weigh them. When measuring liquids, use a clear glass or plastic jug with the metric markings.

We use large eggs with an average weight of 60g.

DRY MEASURES

METRIC	IMPERIAL
15g	½oz
30g	1oz
60g	2oz
90g	3oz
125g	4oz (¼lb)
155g	5oz
185g	6oz
220g	7oz
250g	8oz (½lb)
280g	9oz
315g	10oz
345g	11oz
375g	12oz (¾lb)
410g	13oz
440g	14oz
470g	15oz
500g	16oz (1lb)
750g	24oz (1½lb)
1kg	32oz (2lb)

LIQUID MEASURES

METRIC	IMPERIAL
30ml	1 fluid oz
60ml	2 fluid oz
100ml	3 fluid oz
125ml	4 fluid oz
150ml	5 fluid oz (¼ pint/1 gill)
190ml	6 fluid oz
250ml	8 fluid oz
300ml	10 fluid oz (½ pint)
500ml	16 fluid oz
600ml	20 fluid oz (1 pint)
1000ml (1 litre)	1¾ pints

LENGTH MEASURES

METRIC	IMPERIAL
3mm	⅛in
6mm	¼in
1cm	½in
2cm	¾in
2.5cm	1in
5cm	2in
6cm	2½in
8cm	3in
10cm	4in
13cm	5in
15cm	6in
18cm	7in
20cm	8in
23cm	9in
25cm	10in
28cm	11in
30cm	12in (1ft)

OVEN TEMPERATURES

These oven temperatures are only a guide for conventional ovens. For fan-forced ovens, check the manufacturer's manual.

	°C (CELSIUS)	°F (FAHRENHEIT)	GAS MARK
Very slow	120	250	½
Slow	150	275-300	1-2
Moderately slow	160	325	3
Moderate	180	350-375	4-5
Moderately hot	200	400	6
Hot	220	425-450	7-8
Very hot	240	475	9

index

ARE YOU MISSING SOME COOKBOOKS?

The Australian Women's Weekly Cookbooks are available from bookshops, cookshops, supermarkets and other stores all over the world. You can also buy direct from the publisher, using the order form below.

TITLE	RRP	QTY
100 Fast Fillets	£6.99	
A Taste of Chocolate	£6.99	
After Work Fast	£6.99	
Beginners Cooking Class	£6.99	
Beginners Simple Meals	£6.99	
Beginners Thai	£6.99	
Best Food Fast	£6.99	
Breads & Muffins	£6.99	
Brunches, Lunches & Treats	£6.99	
Cafe Classics	£6.99	
Cafe Favourites	£6.99	
Cakes Bakes & Desserts	£6.99	
Cakes Biscuits & Slices	£6.99	
Cakes Cooking Class	£6.99	
Caribbean Cooking	£6.99	
Casseroles	£6.99	
Casseroles & Slow-Cooked Classics	£6.99	
Cheap Eats	£6.99	
Cheesecakes: baked and chilled	£6.99	
Chicken	£6.99	
Chinese and the foods of Thailand, Vietnam, Malaysia & Japan	£6.99	
Chinese Cooking Class	£6.99	
Chocs & Treats	£6.99	
Cookies & Biscuits	£6.99	
Cooking Class Cake Decorating	£6.99	
Cupcakes & Fairycakes	£6.99	
Detox	£6.99	
Dinner Lamb	£6.99	
Dinner Seafood	£6.99	
Easy Comfort Food	£6.99	
Easy Curry	£6.99	
Easy Midweek Meals	£6.99	
Easy Spanish-Style	£6.99	
Food for Fit and Healthy Kids	£6.99	
Foods of the Mediterranean	£6.99	
Foods That Fight Back	£6.99	
Fresh Food Fast	£6.99	
Fresh Food for Babies & Toddlers	£6.99	
Good Food for Babies & Toddlers	£6.99	
Great Kids' Cakes	£6.99	
Greek Cooking Class	£6.99	
Grills	£6.99	
Healthy Heart Cookbook	£6.99	
Indian Cooking Class	£6.99	
Japanese Cooking Class	£6.99	

TITLE	RRP	QTY
Just For One	£6.99	
Just For Two	£6.99	
Kids' Birthday Cakes	£6.99	
Kids Cooking	£6.99	
Kids' Cooking Step-by-Step	£6.99	
Low-carb, Low-fat	£6.99	
Low-fat Food for Life	£6.99	
Main Course Salads	£6.99	
Mexican	£6.99	
Middle Eastern Cooking Class	£6.99	
Midweek Meals in Minutes	£6.99	
Mince in Minutes	£6.99	
Mini Bakes	£6.99	
Moroccan & the Foods of North Africa	£6.99	
Muffins, Scones & Breads	£6.99	
New Casseroles	£6.99	
New Curries	£6.99	
New Entertaining	£6.99	
New French Food	£6.99	
New Salads	£6.99	
One Pot	£6.99	
Party Food and Drink	£6.99	
Pasta Meals in Minutes	£6.99	
Quick & Simple Cooking	£6.99	
Rice & Risotto	£6.99	
Salad Days	£6.99	
Saucery	£6.99	
Sauces Salsas & Dressings	£6.99	
Sensational Stir-Fries	£6.99	
Simple Healthy Meals	£6.99	
Simple Starters Mains & Puds	£6.99	
Slim	£6.99	
Soup	£6.99	
Stir-fry	£6.99	
Tapas Mezze Antipasto & other bites	£6.99	
Thai Cooking Class	£6.99	
Traditional Italian	£6.99	
Vegetarian Meals in Minutes	£6.99	
Vegie Food	£6.99	
Vegie Stars	£6.99	
Wicked Sweet Indulgences	£6.99	
Wok Meals in Minutes	£6.99	
TOTAL COST	£	

Mr/Mrs/Ms _____

Address_____ Postcode_____

Day time phone _____ email* (optional) _____

I enclose my cheque/money order for £ _____

or please charge £ _____

to my: ☐ Access ☐ Mastercard ☐ Visa ☐ Diners Club

Card number | | | | | | | | | | | | | | | | |

Expiry date _____ 3 digit security code *(found on reverse of card)* _____

Cardholder's name_____ Signature _____

To order: Mail or fax – photocopy or complete the order form above, and send your credit card details or cheque payable to: Australian Consolidated Press (UK), ACP Books, 10 Scirocco Close, Moulton Park Office Village, Northampton NN3 6AP. phone (+44) (0)1604 642200 fax (+44) (0)1604 642300 email books@acpuk.com or order online at www.acpuk.com
Non-UK residents: We accept the credit cards listed on the coupon, or cheques, drafts or International Money Orders payable in sterling and drawn on a UK bank. Credit card charges are at the exchange rate current at the time of payment. **Postage and packing UK:** Add £1.00 per order plus £1.75 per book. **Postage and packing overseas:** Add £2.00 per order plus £3.50 per book. All pricing current at time of going to press and subject to change/availability.
* By including your email address, you consent to receipt of any email regarding this magazine, and other emails which inform you of ACP's other publications, products, services and events, and to promote third party goods and services you may be interested in.

TEST KITCHEN
Food director Pamela Clark
Test Kitchen manager + nutritional information Belinda Farlow
ACP BOOKS
General manager Christine Whiston
Editorial director Susan Tomnay
Creative director Hieu Chi Nguyen
Designer Hannah Blackmore
Senior editor Wendy Bryant
Additional text Kylie Boyd
Director of sales Brian Cearnes
Marketing manager Bridget Cody
Business analyst Rebecca Varela
Operations manager David Scotto
Production manager Victoria Jefferys
International rights enquiries Laura Bamford
lbamford@acpuk.com

acp books

ACP Books are published by ACP Magazines a division of PBL Media Pty Limited
Group publisher, Women's lifestyle Pat Ingram
Director of sales, Women's lifestyle Lynette Phillips
Commercial manager, Women's lifestyle Seymour Cohen
Marketing director, Women's lifestyle Matthew Dominello
Public relations manager, Women's lifestyle Hannah Deveraux
Creative director, Events, Women's lifestyle Luke Bonnano
Research Director, Women's lifestyle Justin Stone
ACP Magazines, Chief Executive officer Scott Lorson
PBL Media, Chief Executive officer Ian Law

Produced by ACP Books, Sydney.
Published by ACP Books, a division of ACP Magazines Ltd, 54 Park St, Sydney; GPO Box 4088, Sydney, NSW 2001.
phone (02) 9282 8618 fax (02) 9267 9438.
acpbooks@acpmagazines.com.au
www.acpbooks.com.au
Printed by Dai Nippon in Korea.

Australia Distributed by Network Services, phone +61 2 9282 8777 fax +61 2 9264 3278 networkweb@networkservicescompany.com.au
United Kingdom Distributed by Australian Consolidated Press (UK), phone (01604) 642 200 fax (01604) 642 300 books@acpuk.com
New Zealand Distributed by Netlink Distribution Company, phone (9) 366 9966 ask@ndc.co.nz
South Africa Distributed by PSD Promotions, phone (27 11) 392 6065/6/7 fax (27 11) 392 6079/80 orders@psdprom.co.za
Canada Distributed by Publishers Group Canada, phone (800) 663 5714 fax (800) 565 3770 service@raincoast.com

Title: Salad days : the Australian women's weekly/ food director, Pamela Clark.
ISBN: 978 1 86396 747 1 (pbk.)
Notes: Includes index.
Subjects: Salads.
Other Authors/Contributors: Clark, Pamela.
Also Titled: Australian women's weekly.
Dewey Number: 641.83
© ACP Magazines Ltd 2008
ABN 18 053 273 546

Scanpan cookware is used in the AWW Test Kitchen. The publishers would like to thank the following for props used in photography: Spotlight, Universal Enterprises, Major and Tom, Rhubarb, Maxwell & Williams, Robert Gordon Australia and Mud Australia.
Send recipe enquiries to: askpamela@acpmagazines.com.au